IT Project+ CoursePrep ExamGuide

Kathy Schwalbe, Ph.D., PMP

COURSE TECHNOLOGY

THOMSON LEARNING

Australia • Canada • Mexico • Singapore • Spain • United Kingdom • United States

COURSE TECHNOLOGY
THOMSON LEARNING

IT Project+ CoursePrep ExamGuide by Kathy Schwalbe, Ph.D., PMP
is published by Course Technology

Managing Editor:
Jennifer Locke

Marketing Manager:
Toby Shelton

Editorial Assistant:
Janet Aras

Production Editor:
Danielle Power

Manufacturing Manager:
Denise Sandler

Internal Design:
GEX Publishing Services

Cover Design:
Betsy Young and
Julie Malone

Compositor:
GEX Publishing Services

TABLE OF CONTENTS

PREFACE

IT Project+ CoursePrep ExamGuide is the very best tool to use to prepare for exam day. It provides thorough preparation for CompTIA's IT Project+ certification exam. CoursePrep ExamGuide provides you ample opportunity to practice, drill and rehearse for the exam!

The IT Project+ CoursePrep ExamGuide provides the essential information you need to master each exam objective. The ExamGuide workbook format devotes an entire two-page spread to each certification objective for the IT Project+ exam, helping you to understand the objective, and giving you the "bottom line" information—what you *really* need to know. Memorize these facts and bulleted points before heading into the exam. In addition, there are seven practice-test questions for each objective on the right-hand page: that's over 600 questions total! CoursePrep ExamGuide provides the exam fundamentals and gets you up to speed quickly.

FEATURES

The *IT Project+ CoursePrep ExamGuide* includes the following features:

List of domains and objectives taken directly from the CompTIA Web site The book is divided into the four IT Project+ domains. The objectives under each domain are found within the sections. For more information about the IT Project+ Exam, visit CompTIA's Web site at *www.comptia.org.*

Detailed coverage of the certification objectives in a unique two-page spread Study strategically by really focusing in on the certification objectives. To enable you to do this, a two-page spread is devoted to each certification objective. The left-hand page provides the critical facts you need, while the right-hand page features practice questions relating to that objective. You'll find that the certification objective(s) and sub-objectives(s) are clearly listed in the upper left-hand corner of each spread.

An overview of the objective is provided in the ***Understanding the Objective*** section. Next, ***What You Really Need to Know*** lists bulleted, succinct facts, skills, and concepts about the objective. Memorizing these facts will be important for your success when taking the exam. ***Objectives on the Job*** places the objective in an industry perspective, and tells you how you can expect to utilize the objective on the job. This section also provides troubleshooting information.

Practice Test Questions Each right-hand page contains seven practice test questions designed to help you prepare for the exam by testing your skills, identifying your strengths and weaknesses, and demonstrating the subject matter you will face on the exam and how it will be tested. These questions are written in a similar fashion to real IT Project+ Exam questions. The questions test your knowledge of the objectives described on the left-hand page. You can find answers to the practice test questions in the back of the book.

For more information: This book evolved from *Information Technology Project Management, Second Edition* (ISBN 0-619-03528-5). Please refer to that book for more in-depth explanation of concepts or procedures presented here.

HOW TO USE THIS BOOK

The *IT Project+ CoursePrep ExamGuide* is all you need to successfully prepare for the IT Project+ Certification exam. This book is intended to be utilized with a core text, such as *Information Technology Project Management, Second Edition* (ISBN 0-619-03528-5), also published by Course Technology. If you are new to this field, use this book as a roadmap for where you need to go to prepare for certification—use *Information Technology Project Management, Second Edition* to give you the knowledge and understanding that you need to reach your goal. Course Technology publishes a full series of CompTIA products. For more information, visit our Web site at *www.course.com/certification* or contact your sales representative.

A Quick Guide to the Domains

Domain I: Scope Definition (27%)

This domain covers the knowledge required to identify and define high-level business requirements for a project, project stakeholders, desired project outcomes, and criteria for determining project success. Domain I includes knowledge required to define a project manager's role and authority, to create a scope document that accurately represents the high-level work required to perform the project, a rough schedule and budget for the project, and information related to building stakeholder consensus and obtaining written approval to proceed with a project.

Domain II: Preliminary/Project Planning (39%)

This domain covers the knowledge and skills required to create a project plan, analyze requirements, perform risk management, prepare project budgets, create a project schedule, develop a work breakdown structure (WBS), estimate project costs, develop a communication plan, organize a comprehensive project plan, and close out the planning phase of a project.

Domain III: Project Execution (29%)

This domain covers the knowledge required to track projects and related issues, manage change control, and perform quality, team, and resource management.

Domain IV: Project Closure (5%)

This domain covers the knowledge required to successfully close projects.

Domain I

OBJECTIVES

1.1 Given a vague or poorly-worded customer request, determine the appropriate course of action in order to generate and refine a preliminary project concept definition, informally determine the business need and feasibility of the project, identify project sponsors, obtain formal approval by the project sponsor, and confirm management support.

DEFINING THE PROJECT CONCEPT, BUSINESS NEED, AND FEASIBILITY, IDENTIFYING AND OBTAINING APPROVAL FROM PROJECT SPONSORS, AND CONFIRMING SENIOR MANAGEMENT SUPPORT

UNDERSTANDING THE OBJECTIVE

A major problem with information technology projects is poor scope definition. It is difficult for customers to state their requirements clearly. Nevertheless, it is very important to identify and define high-level business requirements by creating a preliminary project concept definition. The preliminary project concept definition should include the business need and feasibility of the project. It is also crucial to identify stakeholders' expectations for the project, to obtain formal approval by the project sponsor, and to confirm senior management support for the project.

WHAT YOU REALLY NEED TO KNOW

- ◆ **Stakeholders** are the people involved in or affected by project activities. It is very important for a project manager to identify stakeholders on a project and understand their unique needs and expectations.

- ◆ A **sponsor** provides overall direction and resources for a project. The most important resource on a project is typically people.

- ◆ **Senior managers** are important stakeholders on projects. For projects to succeed, they must have support from senior management. Showing how projects meet business needs helps to build senior management support.

- ◆ A **project concept definition** allows you to document the high-level business requirements in the early stages of a project. It often takes several meetings with stakeholders to define the project concept. It is important to focus on how the project fits in with the overall business strategy.

- ◆ The **project manager** is responsible for managing project activities. The **project team** is assigned to work on the project.

- ◆ The **primary driver** for making decisions on projects should be what can best meet business needs. Many information technology professionals professionals focus too heavily on technical aspects of projects.

OBJECTIVES ON THE JOB

Strong starts are very important for projects. Take the time to make sure everyone understands and agrees upon the business requirements for a project. Get formal project approval from the project sponsor and commitment from senior management.

PRACTICE TEST QUESTIONS

1. **Which of the following are typical project stakeholders? Select three answers.**
   a. the project sponsor
   b. the project customer
   c. the CEO
   d. the project manager
   e. the corporate attorney

2. **A document that describes the business needs for a project is the**
   a. project specification
   b. stakeholder needs analysis
   c. project contract
   d. project concept definition

3. **The person who normally provides overall direction and funding for a project is the:**
   a. project sponsor
   b. project manager
   c. senior manager
   d. CEO

4. **Match the following items their description.**
   Stakeholder   a. Interfaces with customer's senior executives
   Senior manager   b. Assigned to work on project
   Project manager   c. Person involved in or affected by project activities
   Project team   d. Responsible for managing project activities

5. **Two software developers on your project disagree on how to design an important part of a system. There are several technologies and methodologies they could use. What should be the primary driver in deciding how to proceed?**
   a. following corporate standards
   b. following industry standards
   c. meeting business needs
   d. using the lowest-cost approach

6. **You are in the early stages of defining a new project, and it is clear to you that there is no senior management support for the project yet. What should you do? Select two answers.**
   a. Proceed with the project as best you can.
   b. Ask your boss for suggestions/advice.
   c. Work with your project team to clarify the business need for the project and determine which senior managers should be involved.
   d. Cancel the project, since there is no senior management support.

7. **What is the most important project resource a sponsor can provide?**
   a. equipment
   b. people
   c. facilities
   d. signatures

OBJECTIVES

1.2 Given a set of criteria which outlines an enterprise's minimal requirements for a project charter, together with stakeholder input, synthesize a project charter.

CREATING A PROJECT CHARTER

UNDERSTANDING THE OBJECTIVE

To achieve formal recognition of a project, all projects should have some type of charter. A charter is a document that provides direction on the project's objectives and management approach. Key project stakeholders should sign the charter to acknowledge agreement on the need for and intent of the project.

WHAT YOU REALLY NEED TO KNOW

◆ A **project charter** is a document that formally recognizes the existence of a project and provides direction on the project's objectives and management.

◆ Key project stakeholders, such as the sponsor, project manager, and affected functional managers, should sign the project charter to show their agreement on the need for and intent of the project as well as their support for the project.

◆ Key project stakeholders should provide input in developing the project charter.

◆ The project charter should include:
- The project's title and date of authorization
- The project manager's name and contact information
- A brief scope statement for the project
- A summary of the planned approach for managing the project
- A roles-and-responsibilities matrix
- A sign-off section for signatures of key project stakeholders
- A comment section in which stakeholders can provide important comments related to the project.

◆ Project charters can take the form of a letter of agreement, a contract, or a short document created using corporate or other guidelines (see ITPM2e, p. 96-97).

OBJECTIVES ON THE JOB

To gain formal recognition for a project and make sure you have key stakeholder buy-in, develop a project charter for all projects. The project charter should be short, should clearly define the key goals of the project, and should specify who is responsible for achieving them.

PRACTICE TEST QUESTIONS

1. **A document that formally recognizes the existence of a project is a:**
    a. concept definition
    b. WBS
    c. charter
    d. contract

2. **Which of the following should be included in a project charter? Select three answers.**
    a. the project title
    b. date of authorization
    c. termination clause
    d. signatures of key stakeholders
    e. change control procedures

3. **Who should provide inputs into the project charter?**
    a. project sponsor
    b. project manager
    c. project team
    d. all of the above

4. **Which of the following can be considered to be project charters? Select two answers.**
    a. corporate standards
    b. letter of agreement
    c. change authorization
    d. contract

5. **You are leading a large project to develop an ERP system for a large corporation. You know it is important to get the inputs of key stakeholders in developing the project charter, but you are having difficulty arranging times for key people to meet. What should you do? Select two answers.**
    a. Create a draft charter and send it to stakeholders for their comments.
    b. Issue a memo requiring attendance at a meeting, saying that those who don't attend will not have access to the new system.
    c. Ask senior management to assist you in stressing to key stakeholders the importance of this project and of attending the meeting.
    d. Hire an outside consultant to develop the project charter.

6. **Some project charters include a section for comments. Why would you want to include comments? Select three answers.**
    a. to highlight key interests/concerns of stakeholders
    b. to make the charter more informal
    c. to promote buy-in on the project
    d. to verify the handwriting of key stakeholders
    e. to solicit input from stakeholders

OBJECTIVES

1.3   Recognize and explain the need to obtain formal approval (sign-off) by the project sponsor(s) and confirm other relevant management support to consume organization resources as the project charter is refined and expanded.

GETTING FORMAL APPROVAL AND SENIOR MANAGEMENT COMMITMENT FOR PROJECTS AS THE PROJECT CHARTER IS REFINED AND EXPANDED

UNDERSTANDING THE OBJECTIVE

Many information technology projects fail because of a lack executive support (see ITPM2e, p. 38-39). Many projects cross departmental boundaries, involve suppliers and outside consultants, and result in major organizational changes. Due to these conditions, formal approval and commitment from senior management is crucial for projects to succeed, especially as the project charter is refined and expanded and as the project scope becomes clearer.

WHAT YOU REALLY NEED TO KNOW

- ◆ If a project has formal approval from a respected senior manager, other people involved in the project will be more inclined to support the project.

- ◆ Project managers need adequate resources, and senior managers can (or cannot) provide them. Organizations have a limited number of resources, so it is important to make sure your project is of value to the organization and will get adequate resources.

- ◆ Project managers often require timely approval for unique project needs. Senior management can (or cannot) provide this approval.

- ◆ Project managers must have cooperation from people in other parts of the organization and often from external organizations. If certain functional managers or suppliers are not responding to project managers' requests for necessary information or support, senior management can step in to encourage their cooperation.

- ◆ Senior managers can also support projects by mentoring or coaching project managers. Many information technology project managers come from technical positions and are inexperienced as managers. It is important for an experienced senior manager to help develop leadership skills in project managers.

- ◆ Projects often change as goals become better defined. For a project to succeed, managers from all areas affected by the project need to be involved in further defining the project. Because organizations often have many projects and goals to pursue, senior management may need to step in to ensure resources are being allocated effectively.

OBJECTIVES ON THE JOB

Make sure all projects you work on have formal approval and support from senior management. If they do not, ask senior management if the project should be canceled or redirected. Projects are much more likely to succeed when they have commitment from executives.

PRACTICE TEST QUESTIONS

1. **How can you get formal approval for a project?**
   a. Get key stakeholders to sign a project charter.
   b. Get key stakeholders to provide verbal approval for a project.
   c. Require legal agreements or contracts for all projects.

2. **Why is it important to have senior management commitment for a project? Select three answers.**
   a. Senior managers can provide adequate resources.
   b. Senior managers can encourage cooperation from functional managers or suppliers.
   c. Senior managers can issue orders to force cooperation on projects.
   d. Senior managers can mentor project managers to become better leaders.

3. **Why do project requirements need to be refined and expanded?**
   a. Project charters are too high-level to have much meaning, so people often ignore them.
   b. Senior managers don't get involved in projects until after the charter and project concept have been defined, so requirements change and expand.
   c. The nature of project work requires that the scope be refined and expanded to define more detailed work as the project progresses.
   d. The project team is normally not involved in developing the high-level requirements for a project, so the requirements are refined and expanded once the project team is assigned.

4. **Why is it often difficult to get and maintain support for a project? Select two answers.**
   a. There is a limited number of resources available in organizations.
   b. There are usually several important projects occurring at once in organizations.
   c. Many projects are started for political reasons.
   d. Many people do not like to work on projects because of their temporary nature.

5. **Two senior functional managers involved in your project constantly disagree on practically everything. Their animosity toward each other is disrupting project meetings and hurting morale and productivity on your project. Put the following steps in order to show how you could best handle this problem.**
   a. Meet with each manager individually to discuss the problem.
   b. Meet with both managers to discuss the problem together.
   c. Meet with senior management to discuss how to handle this problem.
   d. Discuss the problem with your team members to get their suggestions.

6. **Many information technology projects fail because of a lack of which of the following?**
   a. hard-working staff
   b. suitable technology
   c. executive support
   d. good project managers

OBJECTIVES

1.4   Given a scope definition scenario, demonstrate awareness of the need to get written confirmation of customer expectations regarding the project background, deliverables and the strategy for creating them, targeted completion date, budget dollars available, unacceptable risks, priority of the project, sponsor of the project, predetermined tools or resources, and assumptions that resources will be available as needed.

DEFINING CUSTOMER EXPECTATIONS

UNDERSTANDING THE OBJECTIVE

To meet a customer's needs for projects, you must understand his/her expectations in several areas. Discuss important project information with the customer and document your understandings.

WHAT YOU REALLY NEED TO KNOW

It is important to discuss and document important project information, including:

◆ The background of the project. Background includes a problem/opportunity statement, discussion of how the project aligns with organizational goals and other initiatives, and why the project is being initiated at this time.

◆ The deliverables from the project. A **deliverable** is a product, such as a report or segment of software code, produced as part of a project (see ITPM2e, p. 27). It is important to identify and describe in detail all the deliverables of a project. Who will use the product? What will the product look like and be able to do?

◆ The strategy for creating the deliverables. Are there certain industry standards or methodologies that must be used in creating the deliverables?

◆ Targeted completion date and rationale behind that date. What is driving the project schedule? Is the completion date realistic?

◆ Budget dollars available and basis upon which the budget was determined. How much money has the organization set aside or budgeted for the project? How was the budget amount estimated?

◆ Areas of risks that the project client is or is not willing to accept. All projects have some risks. What risks are not acceptable on this project?

◆ The priority of this project as it relates to all the other projects being done within the organization. Some organizations keep a prioritized list of all projects. Resource allocations are often related to project priority.

◆ The sponsor of the project. It is crucial to know who will provide the overall direction for the project and make high-level decisions.

◆ Any predetermined tools or resources and their availability. Are there specific people, hardware, and so on required for the project? Will they be available as needed?

OBJECTIVES ON THE JOB

Discuss and document customer requirements for projects in critical areas.

PRACTICE TEST QUESTIONS

1. **Which of the following items should be documented to help determine project requirements? Select three answers.**
   a. the project deliverables
   b. the project budget
   c. the organization's business plan
   d. predetermined tools or resources
   e. the project manager's background

2. **A product produced as part of a project is called a:**
   a. project specification
   b. WBS
   c. project product
   d. deliverable

3. **Which information should be documented when describing the background of a project? Select two answers.**
   a. the background of the project sponsor
   b. a problem/opportunity statement
   c. criteria for success of the project
   d. why the project is being initiated at this time

4. **How should you clarify customer requirements and expectations for a project? Select two answers.**
   a. Shake hands after making agreements.
   b. Put requirements and expectations in writing.
   c. Have the project sponsor and other key stakeholders sign important documents.
   d. Require legal contracts to clarify requirements and expectations.

5. **You are leading a project team to install a new network system for a major customer. There are many possible ways to meet basic needs, and you want to clarify what the customer wants to have done. Put the following procedural steps in the correct order.**
   a. Meet with your project team to discuss and document questions and issues related to clarifying requirements.
   b. Meet with your customer's key people to discuss and document more detailed requirements.
   c. Obtain signatures from key stakeholders approving the detailed requirements.
   d. Read current documents describing customer requirements and expectations.
   e. Put agreed-to, detailed requirements in writing.

6. **You are having difficulty getting sign-offs on project requirements. Your project team has become impatient and has decided to continue working without the sign-offs. What should you do?**
   a. Issue a stop-work order on the project until you get the required signatures.
   b. Nothing.
   c. If possible, arrange a prompt face-to-face meeting with the people whose signatures you need, and get them.
   d. Report this problem immediately to senior management.

OBJECTIVES

1.5   Given a project scope definition scenario, including a confirmed high-level scope definition and project justification, demonstrate the ability to identify and define the project stakeholders and an all-inclusive set of requirements.

IDENTIFYING AND DEFINING STAKEHOLDERS AND DEVELOPING AN ALL-INCLUSIVE SET OF PROJECT REQUIREMENTS

UNDERSTANDING THE OBJECTIVE

An important skill of a project manager is the ability to assess different situations, people, and project needs in order to identify and define important ingredients for a successful project. Projects are done by and for people, so it is crucial to identify the right project stakeholders. It is also crucial to define and develop the project scope or requirements as clearly as possible.

WHAT YOU REALLY NEED TO KNOW

◆ It is very important for a project manager to make sure that the correct stakeholders are identified. A **stakeholder analysis** is a tool for identifying stakeholders and how best to work with them. It is a matrix that lists key project stakeholders and their organizations, their roles on the project, unique facts about them, their level of interest, their level of influence, and suggestions on managing relationships with them (see ITPM2e, p. 67).

◆ In addition to obvious stakeholders (sponsor, project team, senior management), it is critical to identify and work well with the end users of information technology projects as well as other impacted parties, both internal and external to the organization. For example, suppliers for project deliverables are stakeholders, as are project managers within the organization who are competing for resources.

◆ In defining project requirements, it is important to develop a comprehensive set of requirements that is presented in specific, definitive terms, including the following:

- Differentiation of mandatory versus optional requirements. Documentation should clearly show what must be done and what is optional.

- Success criteria upon which the deliverable will be measured. Is leaving boxed computers on a loading dock satisfactory delivery, or do the computers need to be unpacked and operating on each user's desk?

- Completion criteria. How does the team know when an information technology project is complete? Is it complete when the new system is live for three months, or when it has passed a user acceptance test?

- Requirements that are excluded from the project. It often helps to clarify what needs to be done by also stating what does not need to be done.

OBJECTIVES ON THE JOB

Knowing who key stakeholders are on a project is crucial to success, as is clearly stating the project scope via detailed requirements.

PRACTICE TEST QUESTIONS

1. **Which of the following would be considered to be external stakeholders for a corporate project? Select two answers.**
   a. the government
   b. suppliers
   c. corporate senior managers
   d. the corporate attorney

2. **The end users for your project have had very little involvement in defining the requirements for a new system. You have tried to get them more involved, but they say they are too busy. What could you do? Select two answers.**
   a. Have your project team draft the detailed requirements and minimize the amount of time the end users would need to spend on the project.
   b. Speak to senior management and insist that several end users be assigned to the project full-time.
   c. Use techniques such as prototyping to help get user input and involvement.
   d. Postpone the project until the end users have more time to work on it.

3. **What is the difference between a mandatory requirement and an optional requirement?**
   a. A mandatory requirement must be met or there would be severe negative consequences.
   b. An optional requirement must be met or there would be severe negative consequences.
   c. A mandatory requirement is included in the project's main budget, while an optional requirement is paid for using additional funds.

4. **Your project team just delivered a report as required in your contract. The customer, however, is unhappy with the report because it is very short and does not include the expected level of analysis. How can you avoid this problem in the future? Select two answers.**
   a. Clearly define contents of deliverables, including reports.
   b. Ask the customer to draft the reports ahead of time.
   c. Charge customers by the hour for all reports.
   d. Define success criteria upon which deliverables will be measured.

5. **Your contract states that you have completed your project when the system has passed the user's acceptance testing. Users signed off on the acceptance tests, but now your customer expects you to maintain staff in a help-desk capacity for the next three months. What should you do? Select two answers.**
   a. Request a change to the contract so you will be paid for these new services.
   b. Provide the help-desk service to keep your customer happy.
   c. Discuss this problem with your customer and work out a mutually agreeable solution.
   d. Outsource the additional work to another supplier.

OBJECTIVES

1.5 cont. Given a project scope definition scenario, including a confirmed high-level scope definition and project justification, demonstrate the ability to identify and define the targeted completion date, the anticipated budget, the priorities assigned to scope, time, and cost goals, and key project assumptions.

IDENTIFYING AND DEFINING TARGETED COMPLETION DATE; ANTICIPATED BUDGET; PRIORITIES OF SCOPE, TIME, AND COST GOALS; AND KEY ASSUMPTIONS

UNDERSTANDING THE OBJECTIVE

In addition to understanding project stakeholders and the scope or requirements for a project, it is critical that the project manager clearly identify and define the project's time and cost goals. The project manager must also ascertain the project client's priorities for scope, time, and cost goals and understand the assumptions related to meeting project goals.

WHAT YOU REALLY NEED TO KNOW

- ◆ All projects are finite by definition, so it is crucial that the targeted completion date for a project and the consequences of not meeting it be clearly defined.
- ◆ Some projects have a set completion date regardless of the project's start date, and others are driven by start dates. Project managers must understand the nature of the project's completion date and how it should be expressed (for example, as a specific date in month/day/year format, as a range of dates, or as a specific quarter and year).
- ◆ Project managers should also understand the anticipated budget for a project, including any plus or minus tolerance, contingency funds or management reserves.
- ◆ **Contingency funds** are dollars above the project cost estimate available to reduce the risk of an overrun. For example, a project may be estimated to cost $1 million, but $1.1 million may be in the budget. The additional $0.1 million is contingency funds.
- ◆ **Management reserves** are funds held by the project sponsor that can be allocated to various projects on the basis of need.
- ◆ Project managers should understand the consequences if the project budget is not met. In some cases, there are no additional funds and the scope must be changed. In other cases, additional funds may be available.
- ◆ It is very difficult to meet scope, time, and cost goals exactly as planned for information-technology projects. It is important for project managers to understand the priorities of these three goals when making project decisions.
- ◆ In order to define project goals, assumptions must be made. Project managers should clearly articulate these assumptions.

OBJECTIVES ON THE JOB

Project success is often defined by meeting scope, time, and cost goals. It is crucial for a project manager to understand these goals and their priorities.

PRACTICE TEST QUESTIONS

1. **By definition, projects are which of the following?**
   a. finite
   b. flexible
   c. indefinite
   d. ongoing

2. **Which of the following statements concerning project end dates are true? Select three answers.**
   a. The targeted completion can be a firm date expressed in month, day, year format.
   b. The targeted completion can depend on the start date.
   c. The targeted completion can be ongoing.
   d. The targeted completion can be a range of dates.

3. **Dollars available to reduce the risk of an overrun that are included in a project cost estimate are called:**
   a. management reserves
   b. contingency funds
   c. fudge factors
   d. risk-reduction funds

4. **For a project to be successful, the project manager should strive to understand and meet certain goals. What are the three main project goals to be met?**
   a. scope or performance goals
   b. time goals
   c. political goals
   d. cost goals

5. **Which of the following situations demonstrate the importance of knowing the priorities of project goals? Select two answers.**
   a. There may be negative consequences for not meeting the project budget, such as project cancellation.
   b. The project products may be useless if they are not delivered by a certain date.
   c. The project sponsor might not be available for a key meeting.
   d. The project users may be unhappy if optional requirements are not met.

6. **You are midway through a one-year project, and your project sponsor insists that the project deliverables must be provided exactly as specified, on time and within budget. The project involves complex software development, and you were initially required to use all internal developers on the project. Two of your best developers just quit. What should you do?**
   a. Meet with the project sponsor to discuss options, citing the assumption that only internal developers can be used.
   b. Ask all of your other developers to work overtime without pay to meet project goals.
   c. Minimize scope requirements to finish on time and within budget.
   d. Cancel the project, since the sponsor's requests are impossible to meet.

OBJECTIVES

1.6   Given a project scope definition scenario, including the client's highest priority among quality, time, and budget goals, estimate the potential impact of satisfying the client's highest priority at the expense of the other two, develop a worse case scenario targeted completion date, budget, and quality-level, and estimate confidence in meeting project goals.

ASSESSING THE IMPACT OF SATISFYING THE CLIENT'S HIGHEST-PRIORITY GOALS AT THE EXPENSE OF THE OTHER TWO, PREPARING WORSE-CASE SCENARIOS, AND ASSESSING CONFIDENCE IN MEETING PROJECT GOALS

UNDERSTANDING THE OBJECTIVE

Project managers must manage scope, time, and cost goals for projects. These three often-competing goals are known as the triple constraint of project management. Project managers must assess which goals are most important and understand the relationships among these goals.

WHAT YOU REALLY NEED TO KNOW

- The **triple constraint** involves balancing a project's scope, time, and cost goals.
- Some references refer to meeting quality goals instead of scope goals because quality is an important consideration related to scope.
- All projects should have target scope, time, and cost goals, but normally one or two of these goals are most important. A project to build a new system in support of a special marketing promotion might have time as its most important goal since the system may be useless if it's not delivered on time. Another project might emphasize meeting scope or quality goals, and still another project's most important goal might be cost.
- A change to one project goal often affects other project goals. Increasing a project's scope or quality requirements may require more time and money. Decreasing budget may decrease the amount of work that can be accomplished or the quality of the work. It is important to assess the trade-offs among project goals.
- The project manager should discuss project goals with the sponsor and understand what the highest-priority goals are. If the project team focuses on meeting cost goals at the expense of quality when quality was most important to the client, there will be problems.
- Project teams may develop different scenarios for projects. A worse-case scenario can help you identify potential risks related to the project.
- It is important to include a confidence level along with estimates for project completion dates, budgets, and scope goals. For example, if a project team is only 10% confident in meeting projected completion dates, the project manager may suggest renegotiating the schedule goal.

OBJECTIVES ON THE JOB

Discuss which goal has the highest priority and how these goals are related. Develop confidence level estimates in meeting goals and consider developing a worse-case scenario.

PRACTICE TEST QUESTIONS

1. **Which of the following make up the triple constraint of project management? Select three answers.**
   a. scope
   b. time
   c. human resources
   d. risk
   e. cost

2. **Your project sponsor insists that all project goals must be met and that they are all of equal importance. You know from past experience that this is not the case. Which of the following examples could you use to help explain what it means to prioritize project goals? Select two answers.**
   a. If you lose a key technical or management person on your project, it will affect your ability to meet the scope and quality goals of the project within the current budget and deadline. Would the sponsor be willing to extend the deadline or provide more money for the project, or should the team just deliver the best work it can under these conditions?
   b. Your project customer is extremely demanding. If he/she lowers expectations for quality and require less rigorous reviews of the work, you can do the work faster, but it will cost more money since the project team will do its own internal quality checks.
   c. All project tasks are resource driven. If you put twice as many people on a task, it can be done twice as fast. Will the customer let you hire twice as many people to finish the job in half the time?
   d. If management cuts the project budget by 20%, will the customer cut back on the scope of the project so useful products can still be provided?

3. **One of your developers estimates that he or she is 20% confident of completing an important task for your project on time. Another is 10% confident in his or her time estimate. What is the likely impact on the overall project schedule?**
   a. It is likely that the project will be completed in 20% more time.
   b. It is unlikely that the project will be completed on time.
   c. It is likely the project will be completed on time.

4. **Why would you want to develop a project's worse-case scenario for targeted scope, time, and cost goals?**
   a. Most project sponsors require it.
   b. It can help you identify risks related to the project.
   c. It should provide the basis for your estimates.
   d. It will determine the quality level you provide.

5. **You are managing a software development project for which it is critical to meet the targeted completion date. You have encountered several problems. What are some strategies you might use so you can still meet schedule goals? Select two answers.**
   a. Sacrifice some functionality to deliver a usable product on time.
   b. Outsource the entire project.
   c. Hire more staff to get the work done faster.

1.7   Given a scope definition scenario, recognize and explain the need to investigate specific industry regulations requirements for their impact on the project scope definition and project plan.

INVESTIGATING REQUIREMENTS OF SPECIFIC INDUSTRY REGULATIONS

UNDERSTANDING THE OBJECTIVE

In order to produce quality products, it is important to identify relevant industry regulations. Some products must meet specific quality standards, which will impact the amount of time it takes to do the work. Some software-development projects must follow specific regulations or methodologies, which will also impact scope. These scope requirements will in turn affect the cost and schedule estimates for the project.

WHAT YOU REALLY NEED TO KNOW

◆ Projects are done for different organizations, and organizations often have unique requirements.

◆ Some organizations follow internal standards or methodologies. If you are working on a project that must follow these standards or methodologies, you must consider the impact of doing so on the project's scope.

◆ Some projects must follow external standards or methodologies. For example, government software projects must often adhere to specific regulations. If you are working on a project that must follow these regulations, you must consider the impact of doing so.

◆ Some projects must meet certain quality requirements or standards, such as ISO 9000.

◆ Some projects for certain industries must satisfy specific industry regulations requirements.

◆ It is very important to investigate all relevant standards, regulations, and requirements related to specific products and projects.

◆ Following specific standards, regulations, and requirements will affect project scope.

◆ Scope often increases when there are industry-specific regulations requirements.

OBJECTIVES ON THE JOB

Investigating specific industry regulations requirements as well as other standards or methodologies that might affect a project is an important part of planning for success. These considerations will impact project scope.

PRACTICE TEST QUESTIONS

1. **Which of the following items should you consider when determining project scope? Select two answers.**
   a. internal standards and methodologies
   b. location of the project team
   c. industry-specific regulations
   d. the project manager

2. **Some government projects must follow specific requirements. These requirements are often documented in:**
   a. orders
   b. PERT or Gantt charts
   c. charters
   d. regulations or standards

3. **Your project team is trying to determine how much work is involved in writing software for a Department of Defense (DOD) project. The customer requires that all software be written in a certain language and that all development work follow a DOD standard. Your team must also use earned-value analysis for measuring performance. What is the probable impact of these requirements on the scope of the project, compared to not following specific requirements?**
   a. The scope will be decreased.
   b. The scope will be increased.
   c. The scope will be the same.

4. **Your project requires that all software-development work follow DOD standards. What should you include in the scope-of-work to make sure you meet these requirements?**
   a. extra staff meetings
   b. deliverables related to these requirements
   c. outsourcing to a government contractor
   d. earned-value analysis

5. **What quality system standard provides minimum requirements needed for an organization to meet its quality-certification standards?**
   a. the Malcolm Baldrige Award
   b. ISO 9000
   c. X-500
   d. QFD

6. **Your project team has included several tasks related to meeting specific industry regulations. These scope items will probably affect which other aspects of your project? Select two answers.**
   a. equipment
   b. time
   c. facilities
   d. cost

1.8 Identify important roles and responsibilities that should be determined during the definition of project scope, including the role of the customer, major skills required in the project team, the type of team structure, and the role of the project manager.

IDENTIFYING ROLES AND RESPONSIBILITIES IN SCOPE DEFINITION

UNDERSTANDING THE OBJECTIVE

It is important to have a clear definition of the roles and responsibilities of project stakeholders as part of the scope definition process.

WHAT YOU REALLY NEED TO KNOW

◆ Project managers should understand the role of the customers or sponsors and how their roles relate to each other. Project team members need to understand who is in charge of what. Most project managers prefer to have the project customers or sponsors make requests through them, so that the managers can then pass those requests on to the project team.

◆ It is important to define communications procedures. A **communications plan** or **communications management plan** is a document for defining project communications, purposes, recipients, and frequencies.

◆ Since people estimate and accomplish work, it is critical to define the major skills required in the project team. Estimates can vary tremendously, depending on the skills of the team, especially for highly technical projects.

◆ There are several types of team structures (see ITPM2e, p. 34-36).

- Many project teams consist of people in **matrix organizations**. A matrix organization is one where personnel report to both a functional boss and a project boss.

- In a **functional organization**, personnel report to a functional boss (for example, engineering, marketing, information technology, and so on).

- In a **project organization**, personnel report to a project boss.

◆ Project team members can also be consultants or independent contractors who are not employees of the main organization. Project team members can be assigned to projects full-time or part-time. It is often easier to manage people assigned full-time to projects.

◆ The project manager must understand the nature of the project team and his or her responsibilities, accountabilities, and authority. Since people often do not report directly to a project manager, he or she must often use informal authority.

◆ The project manager should also understand the performance appraisal process relative to the project. Does the project manager write appraisals for all team members? Who does the appraisal for the project manager?

OBJECTIVES ON THE JOB

Clearly identify roles and responsibilities for key project stakeholders.

PRACTICE TEST QUESTIONS

1. **In which organizational structure do project team members report to both a project manager and a functional manager?**
   - a. functional
   - b. project
   - c. matrix
   - d. Hybrid

2. **You are attending a meeting to discuss a project's scope, but you notice that very few individuals have been assigned to the project team. Why should you be concerned? Select two answers.**
   - a. You know that the skills of the project team members have a direct influence on defining the scope, time, or cost.
   - b. The people at the meeting are senior managers and technical specialists, so you know they will overestimate everything.
   - c. The scope is defined in great detail, and it may be difficult for team members to understand it.
   - d. The people who will do the work should be involved in deciding how to do it and in providing estimates for time and cost.

3. **What document is used to define the type of project communication, purposes, recipients, and frequencies?**
   - a. a statement of work
   - b. a communications management plan
   - c. a stakeholder analysis
   - d. a project Web site

4. **A functional manager has offered to provide you with either five people full-time for your project or ten people half-time. Which would be easier to manage?**
   - a. five full-time people
   - b. ten half-time people
   - c. it does not matter

5. **What type of authority can you use to influence people to do work on a project if they do not report to you?**
   - a. formal authority
   - b. informal authority
   - c. direct authority
   - d. indirect authority

6. **What information is included in a communications plan? Select two answers.**
   - a. the frequency of communications
   - b. who will receive the communications
   - c. performance appraisal information
   - d. salary information

1.9 Given a proposed scope definition and based on the scope components, assess the viability of a given project component against a pre-determined list of constraints.

ASSESSING PROJECT VIABILITY, GIVEN CONSTRAINTS

UNDERSTANDING THE OBJECTIVE

All projects have constraints, and it is important to understand those constraints and how they will affect the ability to meet project goals. Several constraints are having clear definitions of the project end date, monetary resources, product requirements, completion criteria, defined priorities, cost, schedule, and scope priorities, project ownership, mandated tools, personnel and other resources, vendor or company terms and conditions, a best-practices life cycle for this type of project, and required reviews of deliverables by stakeholders and approvals by sponsors.

WHAT YOU REALLY NEED TO KNOW

- ◆ Projects are done in organizations, and it is important to understand the numerous constraints put on a project by the organization. Some constraints will increase the likelihood of project success, and others may impede success.
- ◆ Some constraints are based on how clearly the project is defined. It is usually more difficult for a project to succeed if scope, time, and cost goals are not well defined. These goals must be realistic and prioritized, too. It is also important to have clearly defined completion criteria and priorities for a project and understand who owns the project.
- ◆ To set the stage for project success, project managers should know whether if there are mandated tools, personnel, and other resources for the project. These mandates will impact estimated scope, time, and cost goals.
- ◆ Many information technology projects suffer from **scope creep**, the tendency for scope to keep getting bigger and bigger (see ITPM2e, p. 107). Some projects attempt to minimize scope creep by including a constraint stating that a project's scope can change only by using approved change control procedures. The project manager must know if there is a requirement that scope will change only per change control.
- ◆ Vendor or company terms and conditions are also important constraints that project managers must understand if projects are to be well managed.
- ◆ Some projects are required to follow a "best practices" life cycle. For example, some software development projects must use specific methodologies, software, or development processes.
- ◆ Some projects require reviews of deliverables by stakeholders and official approvals by sponsors to increase the likelihood of success.

OBJECTIVES ON THE JOB

Review project constraints and understand how they can help or hurt the likelihood of project success. Try to influence constraints to improve the ability to meet project goals.

PRACTICE TEST QUESTIONS

1. **Which of the following constraints normally help improve the likelihood of information technology projects being successful? Select three answers.**
   a. having a clearly defined project end date
   b. using a specific vendor
   c. having clearly defined completion criteria
   d. requiring reviews of deliverables by stakeholders
   e. having a sponsor from outside the organization

2. **Which of the following constraints normally decrease the likelihood of information technology projects being successful? Select two answers.**
   a. using a "best practices" life cycle
   b. not requiring reviews of deliverables by stakeholders
   c. having a clearly defined set of product requirements
   d. not requiring that scope will change only per change control

3. **In discussing the scope of a project, you discover that your team must follow a corporate standard that uses a particular vendor for all networking equipment. You know that this vendor has had recent problems delivering products of high quality on time. What should you do? Select two answers.**
   a. Follow the given constraint and use that vendor.
   b. Raise the issue with the project team and other key stakeholders.
   c. Investigate alternative vendors for the equipment and propose a course of action.
   d. Use a more reliable vendor despite the corporate standard.

4. **Which of the following situations might result in scope creep? Select two answers.**
   a. Your developers show sample input screens to your users, and the users suggest more input screens that were not in the original specifications.
   b. Two of your developers left the company and you must replace them.
   c. A project constraint is to use formal change control procedures.
   d. The specifications for user reports was not well defined.

5. **You have been asked to lead a new project. The project sponsor is very influential in the organization, and he or she tells you to proceed as quickly as possible with the project. You discover that the scope has not been well defined, and project constraints have not even been discussed. How can you convince the sponsor that you need time to work on these items?**
   a. Explain that the likelihood of project success will be much higher.
   b. Explain that corporate standards require documenting scope and constraints.
   c. Explain that "best practices" require documenting scope and constraints.
   d. Explain that you can do this work very quickly.

6. **What is the term used to describe the tendency for project scope to keep getting bigger and bigger?**
   a. scope growth
   b. scope escalation
   c. scope creep
   d. scope expansion

1.10 Recognize and explain the need to obtain formal approval (sign-off) by the project sponsor(s) and confirm other relevant management support to consume organization resources as the project scope statement is being developed.

GETTING FORMAL APPROVAL AND SENIOR MANAGEMENT COMMITMENT FOR PROJECTS AS THE SCOPE STATEMENT IS BEING DEVELOPED

UNDERSTANDING THE OBJECTIVE

Scope statements can be very long and detailed documents, and it takes time and coordination to develop good ones. It is important to understand what type of scope statement is needed for a project and the best way to obtain formal approvals and management support as the scope statement is being developed.

WHAT YOU REALLY NEED TO KNOW

- ◆ A **scope statement** is a document used to develop and confirm a common understanding of the project scope (see ITPM2e, p. 98-99).

- ◆ The scope statement should include a project justification, a brief description of the project's products, a summary of all project deliverables, and a statement of what determines project success.

- ◆ Government projects often include a scope statement known as a **Statement of Work (SOW)**. Some SOWs are hundreds of pages long, particularly if they include detailed product specifications.

- ◆ If a project has formal approval from a respected senior manager at the beginning of the project and as the project progresses, it is much more likely to succeed. Other people involved in the project will be more inclined to support the project if it has formal approval.

- ◆ Senior management commitment is important throughout the life of a project. There are often many issues raised while developing the scope statement, and it is important for senior management to show its support and make good decisions in the best interests of the project and organization.

- ◆ Developing a good scope statement may require significant resources. It is important for senior managers to provide these resources and to continue to support the project as it progresses.

- ◆ Projects may change as goals become better defined and as other changes occur in the organization. It is important for senior managers to ensure that projects continue to focus on meeting organizational goals.

OBJECTIVES ON THE JOB

Continue to get formal approval and support from senior management as projects progress.

PRACTICE TEST QUESTIONS

1. **What document is used to develop and confirm a common understanding of the project scope?**
   a. a stakeholder analysis
   b. a scope statement
   c. a performance statement
   d. a communications plan

2. **Government projects often use what type of document to develop and confirm a common understanding of the project scope?**
   a. project specifications
   b. WBS
   c. project contract
   d. statement of work

3. **Why do you need senior management support as the project scope statement is being developed? Select two answers.**
   a. Senior management must sign off on the scope statement before the team can begin design work.
   b. Senior management must allocate resources to develop the scope statement.
   c. Senior management can help make important decisions regarding project scope.
   d. Senior management must run the meetings to develop the scope statement.

4. **Two software engineers on your project disagree on how to design an important part of a system. There are several technologies and methodologies they could use, and these decisions will affect the project scope statement, which in turn will affect estimates for project completion and budget. What should be the primary driver in deciding how to proceed?**
   a. following corporate standards
   b. following industry standards
   c. meeting business needs
   d. using the lowest-cost approach

5. **You almost finished developing your project scope statement. However, it is clear to you that there is no longer much senior management support for the project. Other projects seem to have priority now in the organization. What should you do? Select two answers.**
   a. Proceed with the project as planned.
   b. Ask your boss for suggestions and advice.
   c. Work with your project team to clarify the business need for the project and determine which senior managers should be involved.
   d. Cancel the project immediately, since there is no senior management support.

6. **Which of the following scope-related documents usually takes the most time and resources to create?**
   a. a charter
   b. a scope statement
   c. a WBS

1.11 Given an incomplete project scope definition, complete or rewrite the definition to reflect all necessary scope components or explicitly state what is included in the project and what is not included.

COMPLETING OR REWRITING A PROJECT SCOPE DEFINITION

UNDERSTANDING THE OBJECTIVE

Even if a project has a scope statement, it may be unclear what work is to be done. The scope must be clear enough to allow estimation of how much it will cost to do the work and how long it will take. It is often very difficult to write a good scope statement, but there are guidelines that list components that should be included.

WHAT YOU REALLY NEED TO KNOW

Necessary components of a good project scope definition include the following:

◆ Project size. Project size can be defined as the number of computers, number of people, number of lines of code, and so on.

◆ Project cost. The total budget for the project should be defined in dollars or other monetary units.

◆ Projected schedule and window of opportunity. The project should have a projected start and end date. Many projects also have a window of opportunity, or time within which the work must be completed for it to be of value.

◆ Stakeholders, their roles and authorities. As described in previous objectives, you must define key project stakeholders and their roles and responsibilities on the project.

◆ The project manager's role and authority. The scope definition should identify who the project manager is and describe his or her role and authority on the project, especially in terms of hiring or assigning personnel and of authorizing expenditures.

◆ Completion criteria. The project scope definition should clearly describe criteria for determining when specific deliverables and the entire project are complete.

◆ Methodologies to be followed. If the project requires the use of specific methodologies, they must be documented.

◆ The scope change control process. It is important to explain how requests for scope changes will be handled on the project.

◆ Mandated tools, personnel, and other resources. The project scope definition should clearly state the requirement to use mandated tools, people, or other resources.

◆ Industry or government regulations that apply to the project.

OBJECTIVES ON THE JOB

Do not accept an incomplete or poor project scope definition. Rewrite it to make sure everyone is clear on the scope of the project.

PRACTICE TEST QUESTIONS

1. **Which of the following are necessary components of a good project scope definition? Select three answers.**
   a. the project size
   b. the performance appraisal process
   c. the completion criteria
   d. the source selection criteria
   e. the scope change control process

2. **Your project team is rewriting a project scope definition to clarify what is or is not included in the project. What are some examples of items that you might document as not being included in a project scope? Select two answers.**
   a. installing hardware and software at certain locations
   b. managing the project details
   c. providing training on the system
   d. reporting project status information

3. **You are managing a project to produce an information system for a new marketing campaign. The system must be ready by a specific date for it to be useful. What will you miss if you do not meet the projected completion date?**
   a. the window of opportunity
   b. the bonus opportunity
   c. the time-to-market opportunity
   d. the profit-sharing opportunity

4. **You have received an incomplete project scope definition. Put the following actions in order of how you should proceed to complete them.**
   a. Hold a final review meeting.
   b. Review the draft with your project team.
   c. Get signatures on the completed scope definition.
   d. Rewrite the draft with your project team.

5. **You estimate that your project team will need at least a month to rewrite the scope definition for a project because it is so unclear. A key project stakeholder thinks it is a waste of time and money to spend so long rewriting these documents. How can you convince him or her that you should do the rewrite? Select two answers.**
   a. Explain that you must rewrite the project scope definition so you can follow the scope change control process.
   b. Explain that industry standards suggest that you take an extra month to rewrite the scope definition.
   c. Explain that having a clear and complete scope definition will help the project execution run more smoothly.
   d. Explain that one dollar spent identifying and fixing problems early in the project life cycle could save hundreds of dollars later.

1.12 Identify possible elements of a requirements change control process in a final project scope definition and the circumstances in which they would be appropriate.

IDENTIFYING THE NEED FOR A REQUIREMENTS CHANGE CONTROL PROCESS IN THE PROJECT SCOPE DEFINITION

UNDERSTANDING THE OBJECTIVE

In addition to clearly defining project requirements, it is also important to evaluate the need for a change control process, should requirements change. This process should include information on how to request a change, how to analyze the impact of the change on the project, and how to obtain additional funds or time to implement the change.

WHAT YOU REALLY NEED TO KNOW

◆ Many information technology projects require a requirements change control process. No matter how well requirements are defined, there are often good reasons for them to change as technology changes, competition increases, and the business environment changes.

◆ Some projects are undertaken knowing that requirements will be developed as the project progresses. There may not be a need for a formal change control process in these cases.

◆ Important elements of a requirements change control process include the following:

- How to request a change. Many projects have specific change request forms that are reviewed by a group known as a Change Control Board (see ITPM2e, p. 75)

- How to analyze the impact of the change. Most changes in requirements also cause changes in time and cost estimates for the project. It is important to understand how one change affects other aspects of the project.

- How to obtain approval for the additional funds or time to implement the change. Many change control forms include estimates of how much additional money or time the change will require. It is also important to define who can approve these additional funds or time.

◆ Not all requirements changes increase costs or time estimates. Some changes can actually decrease costs or time on a project. The requirements change control process should allow for quick decisions on changes that can help achieve project goals faster or less expensively.

◆ Document how changes will be communicated to affected stakeholders.

OBJECTIVES ON THE JOB

Determine whether or not a requirements change control process is needed for projects. If it is, include information about this process in the project scope definition.

PRACTICE TEST QUESTIONS

1. **When should you define a requirements change control process for a project?**
   a. when the first change request is submitted
   b. during the scope definition process
   c. during contract negotiations
   d. after the project manager is selected

2. **What types of information should be included in a requirements change control process? Select three answers.**
   a. how to interpret project specifications
   b. how to request a change
   c. how to analyze the impact of a change
   d. how to obtain approval for additional funds or time to implement the change

3. **What are some of the reasons to expect requirements to change on information technology projects? Select three answers.**
   a. the project manager might change
   b. new technology might be available
   c. competition might change
   d. the business environment might change

4. **What group is often formed to review change requests?**
   a. a corporate standards board
   b. an industry standards group
   c. a business needs board
   d. a change control board

5. **Most changes in requirements also cause changes in which areas? Select two answers.**
   a. corporate standards
   b. project cost estimates
   c. project time estimates
   d. project quality standards

6. **What type of change requests should be expedited on projects?**
   a. high-cost change requests
   b. change requests submitted by senior managers
   c. change requests that can decrease project cost or time estimates
   d. change requests that are received early in the project's life cycle

1.13 Identify strategies for building consensus among project stakeholders. Given a project kick-off scenario, select an appropriate course of action involving negotiation or interviewing strategies, meetings, memos, etc.

IDENTIFYING STRATEGIES FOR BUILDING CONSENSUS

UNDERSTANDING THE OBJECTIVE

Once a project officially starts, it is a good idea to hold a project kick-off meeting. An important goal of this meeting is to build consensus among project stakeholders about the goals of the project and how it will be managed.

WHAT YOU REALLY NEED TO KNOW

- ◆ A **kick-off meeting** is a meeting held at the beginning of a project or project phase, at which all major project stakeholders discuss project objectives and plans.
- ◆ It is often a good idea to start building relationships with project stakeholders before the project kick-off meeting. Preplanning can help the kick-off meeting run more smoothly.
- ◆ Strategies for building consensus include the following:
  - Negotiation: Project managers should strive for a win-win approach to negotiations, in which both parties benefit from decisions. To negotiate effectively, you must understand individual stakeholders.
  - Interviewing strategies: The best way to understand stakeholder needs and expectations is often through interviews. There are several types of interviews, so it is important to evaluate what works best in each situation. Face-to-face interviews are often most effective.
  - Meetings: It is important to have meetings with various project stakeholders to build consensus. It is also important to run meetings effectively (see ITPM2e, pp. 285-286).
  - Memos: Some stakeholders prefer written memos that document discussion, issues, agreements, and so on. It is important to write memos well and choose words carefully.
- ◆ Information technology personnel sometimes neglect the importance of building relationships with project stakeholders. It is important to develop and emphasize this skill within the project team.

OBJECTIVES ON THE JOB

Don't neglect the importance of building good relationships with key project stakeholders. Plan for kick-off meetings so relationships run smoothly.

PRACTICE TEST QUESTIONS

1. **What type of meeting is usually held at the beginning of a project to discuss project objectives and plans?**
   a. a project sponsor meeting
   b. a project kick-off meeting
   c. a project review meeting
   d. a project status meeting

2. **What can a project manager do to help a project get off to a good start? Select two answers.**
   a. Do preplanning before the project officially starts.
   b. Work on building good relationships with project stakeholders.
   c. Read many books and articles about project management.
   d. Draft important project documents him- or herself.

3. **What is the preferred outcome of negotiations on projects?**
   a. a win-lose outcome
   b. a lose-win outcome
   c. a win-win outcome
   d. a win outcome

4. **What are preferred methods for understanding stakeholders' needs and expectations? Select two answers.**
   a. interview stakeholders
   b. send memos to stakeholders
   c. send e-mails to stakeholders
   d. hold face-to-face meetings

5. **You are just beginning a kick-off meeting for a large corporate project. One of the functional managers immediately raises concerns about the timing of this project and his/her personal opposition to the project. What should you do? Select two answers.**
   a. Ask the manager to restrain him- or herself and go on with the agenda as planned.
   b. Acknowledge the concerns and explain the business need for the project.
   c. Acknowledge the concerns and explain the importance of the timing of the project.
   d. Acknowledge the concerns and go on with the agenda as planned.

6. **You are halfway through a two-hour project kick-off meeting. You notice that several important stakeholders seem bored. What should you do? Select two answers.**
   a. Proceed with the meeting as best you can.
   b. Ask your boss to take over the rest of the meeting.
   c. Readjust your meeting strategy to make it more interactive and engaging.
   d. Ask one of the bored stakeholders to comment on the project and make suggestions on what he or she would like to discuss at the meeting.

OBJECTIVES

1.14 Recognize and explain the need to build management buy-in and approval into the structure of the project and describe strategies for doing so.

BUILDING MANAGEMENT BUY-IN AND APPROVAL INTO THE STRUCTURE OF THE PROJECT

UNDERSTANDING THE OBJECTIVE

You cannot force management buy-in or approval for a project, but you can structure a project to promote better management support. Project managers should involve senior management in developing project charters and important scope documents, reviewing and approving key project deliverables, and acting as spokespersons/advocates for the project.

WHAT YOU REALLY NEED TO KNOW

◆ Recent studies show that senior management support is the most important factor for success on information technology projects.

◆ There are several ways to get senior management support. Senior managers can initiate projects, guide projects, fund projects, and act as project sponsors.

◆ Project managers can structure their projects to help build and maintain senior-management support by using several strategies:

- Involving management in up-front definitions of the project concept and charter. It is important to get senior management involved in a project as early as possible. Senior managers should be influential in defining the project concept and should sign off on the project charter.

- Involving management in defining and approving project scope. Senior managers should attend important meetings related to scope definition and sign off on important scope-related documents.

- Involving management in reviewing and approving key project deliverables as they evolve. Projects can be structured to require senior management review and approval of project deliverables. This strategy will help to keep management involved in the project and aware of its progress.

- Providing a role for management as spokespersons/advocates for the project, for team-member participation, and for the deliverables. Project managers can ask for one senior manager to act as a spokesperson-advocate for their project. This manager could provide introductory comments at important project meetings, sign important documents, and so on. Senior managers should also be asked to participate in important team meetings and to review important project deliverables.

OBJECTIVES ON THE JOB

Senior management support is crucial to the success of information technology projects. Structure projects to promote senior management buy-in and approval.

PRACTICE TEST QUESTIONS

1. **Which of the following is the most important factor associated with success on information technology projects?**
   a. state-of-the-art technology
   b. a well structured contract
   c. a good project manager
   d. senior management support

2. **What can a project manager do to get management buy-in for a project? Select two answers.**
   a. Have the CEO force senior managers to support the project.
   b. Involve management in up-front definitions of the project concept and charter.
   c. Involve management in reviewing and approving key project deliverables.
   d. Involve the CEO in all project review meetings.

3. **What project roles can senior managers take to show their support for them? Select three answers.**
   a. project sponsor
   b. project spokesperson
   c. project auditor
   d. project advocate

4. **How can a project be structured to promote management support? Select two answers.**
   a. Require a senior manager to provide introductory comments at important project meetings.
   b. Require a senior manager to be a member of the technical team.
   c. Require a senior manager to review and approve key project deliverables.
   d. Require a senior manager to write project progress reports.

5. **You are in the middle of an important project review meeting. The discussions have become very technical, and you notice that your project sponsor looks uninterested. What should you do? Select three answers.**
   a. Ask the presenters to focus on how their work will help meet business goals.
   b. Ask the presenters to raise management-level issues as part of their presentations.
   c. Structure meetings so the sponsor does not have to attend the very technical presentations.
   d. Continue the meeting as planned.

6. **You are in the early stages of defining a new project, and it is clear to you that there is not yet any senior management support for the project. What should you do? Select two answers.**
   a. Review the project charter and scope definition to make sure the project addresses important business needs.
   b. Add a requirement for management sign off on important project documents.
   c. Cancel the project, since there is no senior management support.
   d. Continue the project as planned.

Domain II

OBJECTIVES

2.1 Given an approved project scope document, detailed schedule, and budget information, demonstrate the ability to create a project management plan that illustrates understanding of the roles of stakeholders and includes establishing a project tracking mechanism.

CREATING A PLAN THAT ADDRESSES STAKEHOLDER ROLES AND A PROJECT TRACKING MECHANISM

UNDERSTANDING THE OBJECTIVE

A project plan includes much more than scope documents, schedule, and budget information. It is important to include information concerning the roles of various project stakeholders. Project plans can include a responsibility assignment matrix to help in clarifying these roles. Project plans should also include information on how project progress will be measured.

WHAT YOU REALLY NEED TO KNOW

◆ Stakeholder roles should be documented in a project management plan. There are several ways to document these roles.
- The plan can list the project stakeholders by organization or name, along with specific roles and responsibilities.
- The plan can include a **responsibility assignment matrix**, which maps the work of the project as described in the WBS to the people responsible for performing the work (see ITPM2e, p. 244-245).

◆ As stakeholders or work changes on the project, the project plan should be updated.

◆ It is important to state clearly which stakeholders are responsible for performing specific work, reviewing work, approving work, and so on.

◆ Tracking mechanisms include developing project metrics, using status and progress reports, and using earned value management.
- **Metrics** are ways of measuring performance. Examples of project metrics could include the number of lines of code developed per week, the number of computers installed to date, and so on.
- **Status reports** describe where the project stands at a specific point in time. For example, halfway through a project, a status report would describe how much has been completed to date.
- **Progress reports** describe what the project team has accomplished during a certain period of time. For example, many projects require monthly progress reports that describe what work has been accomplished each month.
- **Earned value management** is a project performance measurement technique that integrates scope, time, and cost data (see Objective 3.7).

OBJECTIVES ON THE JOB

Make sure project plans include information that clearly describes stakeholders' roles on the project. Also include detailed information on how progress will be measured and tracked.

PRACTICE TEST QUESTIONS

1. **Which of the following tools can be used to map the work of the project for use by the people responsible for performing the work?**
    a. a WBS
    b. a Gantt chart
    c. a responsibility assignment matrix
    d. a resource histogram

2. **You are in the early stages of a new project, and you notice that many stakeholders seem confused about their roles on the project. There is some duplication of effort, and other work is not being done. You reviewed the project plan and found little description of roles and responsibilities What should you do? Select two answers.**
    a. Draft a new section for the project plan describing roles and responsibilities and review it with all affected stakeholders.
    b. Issue a stop work order until roles and responsibilities are clarified in writing.
    c. Meet with your project team to develop a detailed resource histogram for every project stakeholder.
    d. Meet with your project team and other stakeholders to clarify roles and responsibilities.

3. **What are some of the roles stakeholders have on projects? Select three answers.**
    a. performing work
    b. reviewing work
    c. outsourcing work
    d. approving work

4. **Match the following items to their descriptions.**

    Metric   a. Measurement technique integrating scope, time, and cost data
    Status report   b. Way of measuring performance
    Progress report c. Describes work accomplished during a certain period of time
    Earned value   d. Describes where the project stands at a specific point in time.

5. **Earned value management integrates what types of data? Select three answers.**
    a. scope data
    b. quality data
    c. cost data
    d. time data

6. **Your project team is developing metrics for your project. The project involves installing thousands of new computers and related off-the-shelf hardware and software in ten different locations. What could you use as metrics? Select two answers.**
    a. the number of computers installed
    b. the number of contracts issued
    c. the number of office installations completed
    d. the number of lines of code developed

OBJECTIVES

2.2 Given a scenario with necessary project documents and resource calendars, demonstrate the ability to develop an initial project schedule by defining and sequencing project tasks, estimating durations for tasks, specifying resource requirements, and determining appropriate schedule formats.

DEFINING AND SEQUENCING PROJECT TASKS

UNDERSTANDING THE OBJECTIVE

Developing a realistic and useful project schedule is a critical part of project planning. The project team must define and sequence project tasks, estimate their durations and resource requirements, and decide how to communicate schedule information.

WHAT YOU REALLY NEED TO KNOW

◆ A **task** or **activity** is an element of work, normally found on the WBS, that has an expected duration, a cost, and resource requirements.

◆ In order to estimate duration and resources required for a task, the project team must first clearly define tasks by developing a more detailed WBS and supporting explanations.

◆ A dependency or relationship shows the sequencing of project tasks. There are three basic types of dependencies:

- **Mandatory dependencies** are inherent in the nature of the work. For example, you cannot test code until after it is written.

- **Discretionary dependencies** are defined by the project team. For example, a project team might decide not to start a detailed design of a new system until users sign off on the analysis work.

- **External dependencies** involve relationships between project and nonproject tasks. For example, the installation of a new operation system and other software may depend on delivery of new hardware from an external supplier.

◆ **Project network diagrams** display the sequencing of tasks. Most project management software displays project network diagrams using the precedence diagramming method where boxes represent tasks and arrows connect related tasks.

◆ The longest path through a project network diagram is called **the critical path**. The length of the critical path is the minimum amount of time required to complete a project (see ITPM2e, p.132-137). If any task on the critical path takes longer than planned, the project completion date will be extended.

OBJECTIVES ON THE JOB

Take time to define project tasks and dependencies clearly. Task definitions and dependencies provide the basis for time, cost, and resource estimates. Use project network diagrams to display task sequencing and determine the critical path.

PRACTICE TEST QUESTIONS

1. **When defining a task or activity, the project team must develop estimates for which of the following items? Select three answers.**
   a. the duration of the task
   b. the cost of the task
   c. the quality standard for the task
   d. the resource requirements for the task

2. **Match the following types of dependencies to a description of each.**

   Mandatory   a. Involves relationships between project and non-project tasks
   Discretionary b. Inherent in the nature of the work
   External   c. Defined by the project team

3. **What tool is used to display the sequencing of project tasks?**
   a. WBS
   b. network diagram
   c. Gantt chart
   d. Pareto diagram

4. **Task A precedes tasks B and C. Task B precedes Task D. Task C precedes Task E. The estimated durations of the tasks are as follows: Task B's estimated duration is 10 days, Task C's estimated duration is 12 days, and all other task estimates are 5 days. Which tasks are not on the critical path? Select two answers.**
   a. Task B
   b. Task C
   c. Task D
   d. Task E

5. **Task A precedes tasks B and C. Task B precedes Task D. Each task has an estimated duration of ten days. How long is the critical path?**
   a. ten days
   b. twenty days
   c. thirty days
   d. forty days

6. **Your project sponsor has asked you to find alternatives for completing the project sooner. Which tasks should you try to complete faster?**
   a. noncritical tasks
   b. critical tasks
   c. the most expensive tasks
   d. the least expensive tasks

OBJECTIVES

2.2 cont.   **Given a scenario with necessary project documents and resource calendars, demonstrate the ability to develop an initial project schedule by defining and sequencing project tasks, estimating durations for tasks, specifying resource requirements, and determining appropriate schedule formats.**

ESTIMATING DURATIONS AND RESOURCE REQUIREMENTS FOR PROJECT TASKS AND DETERMINING SCHEDULE FORMATS

UNDERSTANDING THE OBJECTIVE

To develop a project schedule and cost estimate, you must estimate the durations of tasks and specify resource requirements. There are many ways to communicate schedule information, and it is important to determine what format is appropriate.

WHAT YOU REALLY NEED TO KNOW

◆ A **duration** is the amount of time worked on a task plus elapsed time. For example, if one project task is to develop a user guide and the person creating the guide thinks it will take forty hours to complete the task, but he or she only works twenty hours a week and must wait one week to receive comments, the duration estimate would be three weeks.

◆ Resources assigned to tasks affect duration estimates. It is important to keep resource assignments in mind when making estimates.

◆ There are several ways to communicate schedule information.

- A **Gantt chart** is a standard format for displaying project schedule information by listing project tasks and corresponding start and finish dates in a calendar format. Symbols on Gantt charts display summary tasks, milestones, and so on (see ITPM2e, p.129-130). Most project management software tools create Gantt charts. Gantt charts can be filtered to display all tasks, summary tasks, critical tasks, and so on. Many people like to see project schedules in a Gantt chart format.

- A **network diagram or PERT chart** shows task sequencing. PERT charts can be difficult to understand, so not all stakeholders like to see them.

- **Milestones** are significant project events with zero duration. They are represented by a diamond symbol on a Gantt chart. A milestone report lists milestones and their dates. Senior managers might only want to see milestone reports so that they can keep informed on high-level schedule information.

OBJECTIVES ON THE JOB

Be careful in estimating task durations. Consider resource assignments and elapsed time in making duration estimates. Communicate project schedule information in various ways to meet differing stakeholder needs.

PRACTICE TEST QUESTIONS

1. **When estimating the duration of a project task, which items should you consider? Select two answers.**
   a. the project sponsor
   b. resource assignments
   c. elapsed time
   d. task sequencing

2. **You are halfway through a software development project, yet much less than half the work has been completed. You are reviewing the initial duration estimates for tasks with your software developers. The most senior developer created the estimates. What is the likely cause of the schedule delays? Select two answers.**
   a. The software developers are not properly motivated to do the work on time.
   b. Senior management created unrealistic schedules.
   c. The senior developer did not account for the skill level of resources assigned to do all the tasks.
   d. The estimates assumed senior developers would be doing all the work.

3. **What type of chart or diagram displays project schedule information by listing project tasks and corresponding start and finish dates in a calendar format?**
   a. network diagram
   b. Gantt chart
   c. Pareto chart
   d. Deming chart

4. **Why wouldn't all project stakeholders want to see a network diagram for the project?**
   a. Network diagrams can be difficult to understand.
   b. Network diagrams are not useful for most projects.
   c. Network diagrams show sensitive information.

5. **Which of the following statements is true concerning milestones? Select two answers.**
   a. Milestones can be displayed on Gantt charts and are normally represented by a diamond symbol.
   b. Senior managers often want to see milestone reports.
   c. Milestones durations vary based on the nature of the milestone.
   d. Milestones are often found on network diagrams.

6. **You thought you were doing a good job keeping all stakeholders informed about schedule progress, but the last project review meeting made it clear that people were not reading or understanding the detailed schedule reports. What should you do?**
   a. Impose a penalty for people who don't read their schedule reports.
   b. Ask various stakeholders how they'd like to receive schedule information.
   c. Provide all stakeholders with several formats of schedule information.
   d. Only provide milestone reports, since they are easier to understand.

OBJECTIVES

2.3 Demonstrate understanding of important budgeting concepts, techniques, and issues, including bottom-up cost estimates, standard engineering estimate techniques, and issues to consider when transforming a project cost estimate into a budget.

UNDERSTANDING IMPORTANT BUDGETING CONCEPTS, TECHNIQUES, AND ISSUES

UNDERSTANDING THE OBJECTIVE

There are several ways to develop project cost estimates, and it is important to understand which approach to use for specific projects. Estimates provide the basis for project budgets, which allocate project funds over time.

WHAT YOU REALLY NEED TO KNOW

- ◆ Cost estimating involves developing an approximation of the costs needed to complete a project. Costs often include salaries, hardware, and software.
- ◆ There are several types of cost estimates:
  - A **bottom-up estimate** is based on estimating individual work items and summing them to get a project total.
  - **Analogous** or **top-down** estimates use the actual cost of a previous, similar project as the basis for estimating the cost of the current project.
  - **Parametric modeling** uses project characteristics in a mathematical model to estimate project costs.
  - A **rough order of magnitude (ROM)** estimate is prepared early in the life of a project to provide a general idea of what a project will cost. Experts in a field can often create ROM estimates in a short period of time.
- ◆ There are several techniques for developing standard engineering estimates. Many software development estimates, for example, are based on an estimate of the number of lines of code and a cost per line of code.
- ◆ Project **cost budgeting** involves allocating the project cost estimate to individual work items, and they are usually allocated over time, such as months or years.
- ◆ Organizations have their own ways of budgeting. It is important to translate the project cost estimate into an appropriate format for the organization's budget.

OBJECTIVES ON THE JOB

It is important to have people who understand the project well help in creating the cost estimates. It is also important to understand how to translate the cost estimate into the organization's budgeting process.

PRACTICE TEST QUESTIONS

1. **Which of the following are typical costs included in an information technology cost estimate?**
   a. hardware costs
   b. software costs
   c. salaries for functional managers supporting the project
   d. salaries for project team members

2. **Your project team is developing a cost estimate by estimating individual work items and them summing them up to get a project total. What estimating technique are you using?**
   a. parametric
   b. analogous
   c. delegated
   d. bottom-up

3. **Senior management has asked you to provide a quick estimate of what it will cost to do a major information technology project. They want the estimate to provide a ballpark idea of what it will cost. What should you do?**
   a. Work with your project team for several days to develop a detailed estimate.
   b. Research the competition to find similar projects, then develop a detailed estimate.
   c. Prepare a rough order of magnitude estimate based on your knowledge of the field and expert inputs.

4. **Which of the following is an example of using standard engineering estimates?**
   a. estimating the number of lines of code for a software development project and a cost per line of code
   b. developing a parametric model to estimate project costs
   c. researching similar projects to provide the basis for estimating the cost of the current project
   d. reviewing the organization's information technology budget to develop an estimate

5. **What process do you use to allocate the project cost estimate to individual work items over a period of time?**
   a. cost estimating
   b. cost budgeting
   c. life-cycle costing
   d. net present value analysis

6. **You have developed project budgets several times at your former company. You thought you did a great job of creating the project budget for your new employers, but your colleague in accounting says your inputs are worthless. What could be the cause of the problem?**
   a. The accountant is difficult to work with.
   b. Your new company has an unfamiliar way of preparing project budgets.
   c. Your new company does not follow standard project budgeting processes.

2.4   Identify the characteristics of a formal project quality management plan (e.g., measured quality checkpoints, assignments for architectural control, systems test, unit tests, user sign-off, etc.).

IDENTIFYING CHARACTERISTICS OF A PROJECT QUALITY MANAGEMENT PLAN

UNDERSTANDING THE OBJECTIVE

A quality management plan is intended to document important quality standards that apply to the project and methods by which quality will be assured and controlled. On information technology projects, it is important to give one person responsibility for architectural control, so as to ensure quality throughout the enterprise. There are also numerous tests to ensure quality on projects.

WHAT YOU REALLY NEED TO KNOW

◆ **Quality planning** involves identifying relevant quality standards for each unique project and designing quality into the products of the project. It also involves communicating the correct methods for ensuring quality in a form that is understandable and complete.

◆ **Quality assurance** involves satisfying the relevant quality standards for a project and promoting continual quality improvement.

◆ **Quality control** involves accepting decisions, reworking, and process adjustments.

◆ **Quality checkpoints** are specific points at which quality can be checked. For example, users could test specific functionality or features of a new system to make sure it meets their needs as the project progresses. Users often sign off on specific checkpoints to show their acceptance of work.

◆ Because most information technology projects must work within a larger organizational context, it is important to have someone responsible for ensuring that new systems fit into the overall architecture.

◆ There are several types of tests to ensure quality on information technology projects (see ITPM2e, p. 211):

  - A **unit test** is done to assess each individual component (often a program) to ensure it is as defect-free as possible.

  - **Integration testing** occurs between unit and system testing to test functionally grouped components. It ensures that subset(s) of the entire system work together.

  - **System testing** tests the entire system as one entity.

  - **User acceptance testing** is an independent test performed by end users prior to accepting the delivered system.

OBJECTIVES ON THE JOB

Document quality requirements and plans for projects in a quality management plan. Be sure to define quality checkpoints and tests required for the project.

PRACTICE TEST QUESTIONS

1. **Which of the following processes involves satisfying the relevant quality standards for a project?**
   a. quality planning
   b. quality assurance
   c. quality control
   d. quality checkpoints

2. **Which of the following processes involves acceptance decisions, reworking, and process adjustments?**
   a. quality planning
   b. quality assurance
   c. quality control
   d. quality checkpoints

3. **You are nearing completion of the design of a large information technology project when the company's lead architect voices his concerns about using nonstandard software for the project. The software you propose using would be the best choice for this particular project, and using existing standards would increase time and cost estimates. What should you do? Select two answers.**
   a. Develop estimates based on following the existing standards, then seek senior management's decision on which way to proceed.
   b. Continue as planned despite the organizational standards.
   c. Meet with the lead architect to explore alternatives.
   d. Issue a stop-work order on the project.

4. **What type of test is done to assess each individual component (program) to ensure it is as defect-free as possible?**
   a. unit test
   b. integration test
   c. system test
   d. user acceptance test

5. **What type of test is an independent test performed by end users prior to accepting the delivered system?**
   a. unit test
   b. integration test
   c. system test
   d. user acceptance test

6. **Two of your software developers are having difficulties working together. A senior developer has found that individual programs he/she receives from another developer have not been tested, so the integration testing takes much longer than planned. What should you do? Select two answers.**
   a. Remind all developers to do unit testing on individual programs.
   b. Hold a special meeting with all developers to discuss testing procedures.
   c. Fire the programmer who is writing defective code.

OBJECTIVES

2.5   Given a team-building scenario, including a scope definition and WBS, identify selection criteria for particular team members and demonstrate the ability to ask interview questions that will assist the team selection process.

IDENTIFYING SELECTION CRITERIA AND INTERVIEW QUESTIONS
FOR SELECTING TEAM MEMBERS

UNDERSTANDING THE OBJECTIVE

People make or break projects. It is important to select team members who can contribute to successful completion of a project and to spend time building a cohesive, productive team.

WHAT YOU REALLY NEED TO KNOW

◆ People must work together to complete projects successfully. In addition to having strong individuals on a team, project teams must set aside time for team-building activities in order to work together effectively.

◆ After determining the initial scope of a project and developing a WBS, it is important to decide which individuals will do the tasks of the project. The skills required for the task should be defined so that appropriate resources can be assigned.

◆ The most effective way to select new team members or to determine specific resource assignments is by interviewing people. The goal is to match the work to the people most suited for each task.

◆ It is important to develop good interview questions. In addition to asking technical questions to make sure someone knows how to do the work, it is important to ask behavioral questions, also. For example, the following questions provide insight into how someone works in a team environment:

◆ Describe a situation where you had to do a very challenging task that you could not figure out on your own. What did you do?

◆ Describe a situation where one of your project team members was not pulling his or her weight. What did you do?

◆ Describe a project you worked on where the team really clicked. What factors do you think contributed to the team's synergy?

OBJECTIVES ON THE JOB

One cannot overemphasize the importance of people on projects. Try to pick the right people to work on project teams and assign appropriate tasks to the right people. Take time to work on team building throughout the life of a project.

PRACTICE TEST QUESTIONS

1. **What should be the main criteria in assigning resources to tasks?**
   a. minimizing time
   b. minimizing cost
   c. matching the right people to tasks
   d. using whoever is available

2. **Your project team has decided on the initial WBS for a project, and you are trying to assign resources to the main tasks. One very vocal person wants to be in charge of a major subtask. You know that another team member is better qualified to lead that task, but he/she is not saying a word. What should you do?**
   a. Use your authority as project manager to assign the more qualified person to that task, despite the vocal person's objections.
   b. Table the decision on who leads that task and discuss it in a smaller meeting with the people involved.
   c. Ask the quiet person what he/she thinks.
   d. Let the vocal person lead that task.

3. **You need to acquire more resources for your project team. What should you do?**
   a. Ask appropriate functional managers to provide people based on job titles.
   b. Ask the existing team members what friends they have who might want to work on the project.
   c. Develop good interview questions to ask potential resources to see if they would be a good fit for the project.

4. **You have just been asked to take over as project manager on a large information technology project. The project team members have been together for about a year, but you are brand new to the company. You have allocated time for team-building activities, but several people think that is a waste of time and money. What should you do? Select two answers.**
   a. Explain that the team continues to change as people change and that you want everyone to benefit from the team-building activities.
   b. Let people attend on a voluntary basis.
   c. Ask the people opposed to the activities for their comments one-on-one.
   d. Turn the team-building activities into a competition and award prizes for individual contributions.

5. **You are very experienced in using behavioral interviews when hiring new employees or selecting new team members. Your new head of human resources, however, wants you to follow his/her list of interview questions. Time is of the essence. What should you do?**
   a. Use the head of human resources' list of questions.
   b. Meet with the head of human resources and provide a list of proposed questions for his or her approval.
   c. Use your authority as project manager and stick with your own interview questions.
   d. Ask the head of human resources to hire the new employees for you.

2.6   Identify methods for resolving disagreements among team members when evaluating the suitability of deliverables at each point in their evolution.

RESOLVING DISAGREEMENTS AMONG TEAM MEMBERS

UNDERSTANDING THE OBJECTIVE

It is human nature for people to disagree. There are different types of conflict, and it is important to manage conflict in the best interest of meeting project objectives.

WHAT YOU REALLY NEED TO KNOW

◆ There are several conflict handling modes that project managers can use (see ITPM2, p. 281):

- In **confrontation mode**, project managers directly face a conflict, using a problem-solving approach that allows affected parties to work through their disagreements. This approach is normally most effective.

- In **compromise mode**, you use a give-and-take approach to resolving conflicts. People bargain and search for a solutions that bring some degree of satisfaction to all the parties in a dispute.

- **Smoothing mode** is used to de-emphasize or avoid areas of differences and emphasize areas of agreement. This approach is often used when two people have severe personality clashes.

- The **forcing mode** is the same as taking a win-lose approach to conflict resolution. Managers who are very competitive or autocratic might favor this approach.

- In **withdrawal mode**, is when you withdraw from an actual or potential disagreement. Little gets accomplished using this mode.

◆ Not all conflict is bad. **Task-related conflict** often improves team performance because team members discuss different approaches to producing project deliverables and often come up with even better solutions. If team members disagree on how to produce deliverables, the project manager should help them get all options out in the open, brainstorm new ideas, and discuss the best way to proceed.

◆ **Emotional conflicts** or personality clashes and misunderstandings often depress team performance. Project teams should develop group ground rules, including one to avoid emotional conflict. Team members should focus on fixing problems instead of blaming people.

OBJECTIVES ON THE JOB

Realize that people will have differences of opinion on many aspects of projects. Focus on solving problems, not blaming people.

PRACTICE TEST QUESTIONS

1. **Which of the following is the normally the most effective method for handling conflicts?**
   a. confrontation mode
   b. compromise mode
   c. smoothing mode
   d. forcing mode

2. **Match the following conflict handling modes with their descriptions:**

   Withdrawal   a. Using a problem-solving approach to resolving disagreements
   Forcing   b. Using a give-and-take-approach to resolving conflicts
   Smoothing   c. Taking a win-lose approach to conflict resolution
   Confrontation   d. Avoiding an actual or potential disagreement
   Compromise   e. De-emphasizing differences and emphasizing areas of agreement

3. **What type of conflict is good on projects?**
   a. personality clashes
   b. power struggles
   c. task-related conflict
   d. emotional conflict

4. **You are managing an enterprise-wide project. An important functional manager is known for being stubborn and outspoken. This manager has made it known that he/she thinks you are not qualified to be in charge of this project. What should you do?**
   a. Talk directly to the functional manager about the problem.
   b. Issue a memo to all stakeholders citing your qualifications.
   c. Ask your senior manager to intervene.
   d. Ignore the accusations.

5. **Two of the users of your product have major personality clashes. Whenever they are both at a project review meeting, you ask them how their grade-school children are doing. What conflict handling mode are you using?**
   a. confrontation mode
   b. compromise mode
   c. smoothing mode
   d. forcing mode

6. **You are in the middle of a project review meeting when one of your senior technical people accuses another team member of being incompetent. The accused person gets up and leaves the room. What should you do?**
   a. Ask the senior technical person to meet with you after the meeting to discuss the problem.
   b. Apologize for the disturbance and continue with the meeting.
   c. Follow the accused team member out of the room to talk to him/her.
   d. End the meeting.

OBJECTIVES

2.7 Given a project description/overview and list of project requirements: Decide if the project is defined well enough to achieve a measurable outcome and metrics for success. Determine if the requirements include the necessary range of inputs, are related to the project at hand, and are complete, accurate and valid. Recognize the role poorly detailed requirements play in a situation where project outcomes are not possible to verify. Identify the value of the project to the sponsor and users of the outcome. Describe the role of project value and its importance to individual and team effectiveness.

EVALUATING REQUIREMENTS AND PROJECT VALUE

UNDERSTANDING THE OBJECTIVE

Having clear requirements is crucial for project success. It is important for project teams to review project requirements to make sure they are clear and complete. It is also important for requirements to describe measurable outcomes and a product or service that is valuable to the organization. Organizations often determine project value in terms of financial success.

WHAT YOU REALLY NEED TO KNOW

◆ It is important to review requirements and assess whether or not they can help the project team have measurable outcomes and metrics for success. For example, a requirement to provide reports for a system is not specific enough. How many reports? What information is required in the reports? What types of queries will be run to generate the reports? How many simultaneous users will be running the reports? All of these factors should be part of the written requirements for a project.

◆ Requirements should include several characteristics:

- They should include a necessary range of inputs. For example, if a project involves upgrading a new system, the requirements should state what inputs are required for properly testing and operating the new system.

- It is easy for **scope creep** to occur, so it is essential to make sure that requirements are related to the project at hand. New or questionable requirements should be carefully evaluated by the project team.

- Requirements must be complete, accurate, and valid. Users of the products of the project must be heavily involved in defining requirements to ensure their completeness and accuracy. Testing can help ensure validity of requirements.

◆ Many information technology projects are expensive and resource intensive. It is important to understand and communicate the value of the project to the organization and project team.

OBJECTIVES ON THE JOB

Carefully review project requirements to make sure they describe measurable outcomes and will lead to developing products or services that are valuable to the organization.

PRACTICE TEST QUESTIONS

1. **Your team is reviewing the requirements description for a major product you must produce as part of your project. Everyone involved has questions about what the customers really want, and there are many different views on what will meet the stated requirements. What should you do? Select two answers.**
   a. Ask the senior members of your project team to rewrite the requirements so they are clearer.
   b. Meet with the customer/users to clarify the requirements in more detail.
   c. Continue as scheduled, focusing on meeting all the stated requirements.
   d. Develop a process for getting continuous user feedback on the product as the project progresses.

2. **You have taken over as project manager for a large software development project. The previous project manager warned you that nobody knew what he/she really wanted from the project, so it was impossible to please anyone. What should you do? Select two answers.**
   a. Meet with key stakeholders to discuss the main goals of the project and how it provides value to the organization.
   b. Ignore the advice and focus on completing the project according to the written contract.
   c. Find out who is paying for the project and focus on pleasing him or her.
   d. Meet with senior management to clarify project goals and what the project sponsor viewed as a successful outcome.

3. **One of your developers has been working hard for two weeks to get a special function to work. When you check the requirements, you do not find any mention of this function. The developer said one of the users asked for it. What should you do?**
   a. Review the project's process for defining and assigning work to make sure the team focuses on important project requirements.
   b. Praise the developer for being so responsive to users and suggest that others follow his or her lead.
   c. Continue managing the project as planned.

4. **How do most organizations measure the value of projects?**
   a. financial success for the organization
   b. a positive outcome at the final project meeting
   c. obtaining follow-on projects
   d. minimizing scope creep

5. **You have been working on a project for over a year, and requirements seem to change weekly. No one is sure what work to do, and the targeted completion date continues to slip, but no one seems to mind. What are some likely causes of this situation? Select two answers.**
   a. The project is not a high priority.
   b. The organization is poorly managed.
   c. The project team is incompetent.
   d. The project team is understaffed.

2.8   Describe the goals of a useful program requirements review with the client (e.g., verify mutual understanding of client's product delivery, product performance, and budget requirements, etc.) and describe when it is important to have such reviews.

PROGRAM REQUIREMENTS REVIEWS AND WHEN TO HAVE THEM

UNDERSTANDING THE OBJECTIVE

One of the most effective ways to keep projects on track is by having requirements reviews. A project should successfully pass through various phases before continuing to the next. Phases vary by product, but many information technology projects include phases for planning, analysis, design, implementation, and support. Reviews should be held periodically (i.e., monthly or quarterly) and at critical decision points. For example, if requirements are not clear, products are delivered late, or the budget changes, a special review is needed.

WHAT YOU REALLY NEED TO KNOW

- ◆ It is important to take time to review program requirements and the way the project is going.
- ◆ Most reviews are held face-to-face with affected stakeholders in attendance. Face-to-face reviews allow people to communicate most effectively. Some reviews can be done using other methods.
- ◆ Reviews should emphasize important project goals:
  - Does everyone understand the main goals of the project?
  - Are products being delivered on time?
  - Is the quality of the products acceptable?
  - Is the project proceeding according to budget?
- ◆ Most project plans include a requirement to hold reviews. Reviews are often scheduled on a periodic basis, such as monthly or quarterly. Reviews can also be held as needed when important decisions must be made. Some reasons to hold nonperiodic reviews include:
  - The organization has gone through major changes that may affect the need for the project or requirements of the deliverables.
  - There are misunderstandings related to what the client wants in project deliverables.
  - Products produced during the project do not meet client expectations.
  - The project is significantly over or under budget.

OBJECTIVES ON THE JOB

Make sure projects include periodic reviews of requirements. Also hold reviews as needed to help ensure the project meets organizational goals.

PRACTICE TEST QUESTIONS

1. **What should project plans include to help ensure a mutual understanding of client needs throughout the life of a project?**
   a. internal standards and methodologies
   b. collocation of users and developers
   c. industry-specific regulations requirements
   d. requirements reviews

2. **What should requirements reviews emphasize? Select three answers.**
   a. the main goals of the project
   b. Gantt charts
   c. product quality
   d. budget requirements

3. **Which of the following situations would merit the need for a special requirements review meeting? Select two answers.**
   a. The customer is complaining about the performance of specific products recently delivered for the project.
   b. The budget for the project has been cut in half.
   c. The project team has decided to use new project management software to assist in managing the project.
   d. Several project team members are unclear on important requirements for the project.

4. **You just received a call from a major project stakeholder complaining that the wrong brand of computers was delivered. The computers were also left in boxes in an office, when the client thought they would be set up and running as part of the delivery. You read the requirements in your contract, which do not specify the brand of computer or that they had to be set up as part of delivery. What should you do?**
   a. Listen to the stakeholder, but then explain that you did what was stated in the contract and did not need to do more.
   b. Talk to the stakeholder to understand his/her concerns, then try to develop a solution.
   c. Pass the problem on to your senior management.

5. **You know that it is important to have several requirements reviews on your project. However, many of the project stakeholders are in different locations. What should you do? Select two answers.**
   a. Schedule face-to-face reviews every quarter, giving everyone plenty of lead time to plan for attendance.
   b. Budget for using technology such as Web or video conferencing.
   c. Do not schedule periodic reviews and just hold them on an as needed basis.
   d. Make extensive use of written reports to communicate information, instead of face-to-face meetings.

2.9 Given the client's approved project requirements and the input of stakeholders, decompose these requirements into business and functional requirements while maintaining traceability within strict configuration control.

DECOMPOSING REQUIREMENTS WHILE MAINTAINING TRACEABILITY AND CONFIGURATION CONTROL

UNDERSTANDING THE OBJECTIVE

The project team must decompose requirements into more detail, describing both business and functional needs. It is also important to be able to trace requirements as products are developed and to ensure configuration control.

WHAT YOU REALLY NEED TO KNOW

◆ **Decomposing** requirements means breaking them down into logical groups, then breaking those groups into more detail. A **WBS** is used for this decomposition.

◆ **Business requirements** emphasize business needs. For example, a business requirement might require delivering a product by a certain date so it is available for a preplanned event that is important to the business.

◆ **Functional requirements** emphasize what products or services are required. For example, a new software module might include a functional requirement to have an input screen for entry of specific types of information.

◆ **Technical requirements** emphasize how products or services work. For example, a project might require use of a specific programming language or hardware platform as a technical requirement.

◆ **Traceability** means that you can track a requirement back to documented needs. Some work may be questioned, so it is important to be able to trace the work back to the documented requirements.

◆ **Configuration management** ensures that the descriptions of the project's products are correct and complete. It emphasizes management of technology by identifying and controlling the functional and physical design characteristics of products and their support documentation.

◆ Configuration management specialists identify and document the functional and physical characteristics of products, control any changes to such characteristics, record and report the changes, and audit the products to verify conformance to requirements (see ITPM2e, p. 75).

OBJECTIVES ON THE JOB

Break down requirements to describe business and functional requirements. Provide processes for traceability and configuration control.

PRACTICE TEST QUESTIONS

1. **What tool is used to clarify and decompose tasks?**
   a. Gantt chart
   b. scope statement
   c. PERT chart
   d. WBS

2. **Match the following type of requirements with an example of each.**

Business	a. Provide certain types of screens
Functional	b. Use a specific programming language
Technical	c. Deliver a product by a specific date

3. **You have a detailed WBS for your project. You insist that your project team include the WBS numbering scheme on all documentation. Why would you do this?**
   a. You believe in being detail-oriented.
   b. To provide clearer documentation.
   c. To maintain traceability of the work.
   d. To manage resources effectively.

4. **What can you do to ensure that the descriptions of the project's products are correct and complete?**
   a. Have technical writers on your project team to provide good documentation.
   b. Use configuration management to manage product requirements.
   c. Have detailed requirements reviews on a weekly basis.
   d. Collocate users and developers.

5. **You have been project manager of a project for three months, and your team is working on the user interface. The users have not been very responsive in providing feedback. Which of the following might affect delivery of an acceptable product? Select two answers.**
   a. budget cuts
   b. change of sponsor
   c. change of programming language
   d. increase in number of reviews

6. **Which project team members are responsible for identifying and documenting the functional and physical characteristics of products?**
   a. the project manager
   b. the database analysts
   c. configuration management specialists
   d. technical writers

2.10 Demonstrate the ability to perform risk assessment and mitigation by identifying and prioritizing risks, evaluating the severity of risks, identifying risk on the project's critical path, and determining procedures to reduce potential impacts on schedule.

PERFORMING RISK ASSESSMENT AND MITIGATION

UNDERSTANDING THE OBJECTIVE

Risk is inherent in projects. Project teams should identify the potential risks on their projects and develop a plan for managing those risks.

WHAT YOU REALLY NEED TO KNOW

- ◆ Risk management planning involves deciding how to approach and plan the risk management activities for a project.

- ◆ There are several ways to identify potential risks. Reviewing historical information, analyzing the nature of the project or products, and using various information gathering techniques can help in identifying potential risks.

- ◆ **Qualitative risk analysis** involves assessing the likelihood and impact of identified risks to determine their magnitude and priority. For example, there is always a risk that fire may destroy a building. The project team might identify this risk and note that it would have severe consequences if it occurred but that it is highly unlikely to occur.

- ◆ Risks can be prioritized as high, medium, or low. They can also be prioritized in rank order or by determining risk factors.

- ◆ If any tasks on the critical path take longer than planned, the project will not meet its target schedule date. It is very important, therefore, to understand potential schedule risks for critical tasks.

- ◆ There are several ways to reduce potential impacts of risk on the schedule. Project teams can include **buffers** or additional time before the project completion date to reduce the likelihood of a schedule overrun. Project managers can increase monitoring of critical tasks to help ensure timely completion.

- ◆ **Risk mitigation** is reducing the impact of a risk event by reducing the probability of its occurrence. For example, a project team might decide to use a current version of an operating system instead of planning to user a soon-to-be-released version.

OBJECTIVES ON THE JOB

Information technology projects often neglect risk management. Be sure to identify potential risks on projects and plan how to manage those risks.

PRACTICE TEST QUESTIONS

1. **Which of the following are ways to identify potential risks? Select three answers.**
   a. reviewing historical information
   b. reviewing resumes of project team members
   c. analyzing the nature of the products being produced
   d. brainstorming
   e. analyzing annual reports of suppliers

2. **Which of the following risks would have a high likelihood of occurring but a low impact if they did occur? Select two answers.**
   a. A team member calls in sick for two days.
   b. The project manager has major surgery and needs a month to recuperate.
   c. Lightning strikes your data center.
   d. There are a few grammatical errors in the user guide.

3. **How can you prioritize risks? Select two answers.**
   a. Categorize them as high, medium, or low.
   b. Categorize them as qualitative or quantitative.
   c. Put them in rank order.
   d. Sort them according to who identified them.

4. **Which project tasks have the highest risk of delaying the completion date?**
   a. tasks involving high-risk technology
   b. tasks with buffers
   c. critical tasks
   d. tasks involving software development

5. **Your project sponsor has made it clear that this project must be completed on time or it will negatively affect several other corporate projects. What strategy can your team use to help ensure that you finish on time?**
   a. Add a project buffer.
   b. Apply risk mitigation to all tasks.
   c. Use best practices.
   d. Increase the budget for the project.

6. **What is the term used to describe reducing the impact of a risk event by reducing the probability of its occurrence?**
   a. risk management
   b. qualitative risk analysis
   c. risk prioritization
   d. risk mitigation

OBJECTIVES

2.11 Given a project scope, timeline, cost, project team, and dependencies, demonstrate the ability to create and manage a high-level top-down budget or a detailed bottom-up budget, identify and budget resources, budget for project trade-offs, and install and maintain systems for tracking budgetary expenses against the plan based on existing enterprise systems.

DEVELOPING AND MANAGING PROJECT BUDGETS

UNDERSTANDING THE OBJECTIVE

All projects need some sort of funding, and budgets provide the basis for managing funds. Project managers must be well versed in creating budgets, making budgetary trade-offs, and tracking budgetary expenses.

WHAT YOU REALLY NEED TO KNOW

- ◆ A **budget** is a financial report that documents income and expenses over time.
- ◆ After reviewing other project documentation, such as scope statements, schedules, cost estimates, and resource information, the project team must develop a budget for the project. It is important to understand how the specific organization does budgeting when creating the project budget.
- ◆ Budgets can be developed using a top-down or bottom-up approach, similar to that used in developing cost estimates.
  - A **bottom-up budget** is based on estimating individual work items and summing them to get a project total.
  - A **top-down** budget uses the actual budget of a previous, similar project as the basis for estimating the budget of the current project.
- ◆ It is important to get input from the project team in developing budgets.
- ◆ Human resources are a major part of most project budgets. Funds for personnel must include compensation, benefits, overhead, overtime, and so on. Fully loaded amounts include compensation, benefits, and overhead.
- ◆ Projects often involve several trade-offs that must be made during the course of the project. For example, many projects use goods and services from suppliers, but the specific goods and suppliers may not be known when the budget is created. The project manager can include additional funds in the budget to provide some flexibility.
- ◆ It is very important to track a project's budgetary expenses against the plan and to understand the entire organization's budget. Organizations often take budgets very seriously. For example, a company may limit travel expenses to reduce overall costs, and there may not be funds available if a project team is already over its travel budget.

OBJECTIVES ON THE JOB

Take budgeting seriously. Develop a realistic budget and follow it as carefully as possible.

PRACTICE TEST QUESTIONS

1. **What is used to document income and expenses over time?**
   a. an income statement
   b. a balance sheet
   c. a financial portfolio
   d. a budget

2. **You worked with your project team to prepare a budget, using samples from your former employer. You are several months into your project when you receive a budget report showing that you are running more than 20 percent over your budget for staffing, yet you are right on target according to your estimates. What could be causing this problem? Select two answers.**
   a. The accounting system is flawed.
   b. Your current organization includes additional costs for staff that you did not include.
   c. Your project team members underestimated their hours when preparing the budget.
   d. You did not realize that some of your project team receive paid overtime.

3. **You developed a project budget by using a similar project as the basis for estimating high-level financial information. What budgeting approach did you use?**
   a. best practice
   b. bottom-up
   c. top-down
   d. parametric

4. **What types of cost are usually included in a fully loaded estimate for staffing? Select three answers.**
   a. compensation
   b. benefits
   c. overtime
   d. overhead

5. **Who should be involved in estimating project costs and developing the budget? Select three answers.**
   a. the project manager
   b. the accounting department manager
   c. project team members
   d. people with past experience on similar projects

6. **If the scope is projected to increase on a project, what normally happens to the budget?**
   a. It is automatically increased.
   b. It is automatically decreased.
   c. It stays the same.
   d. It can be negotiated.

2.12 Identify and list the components needed to generate a workable project schedule. Create appropriate project schedules which meet the approved project start and finish dates, given a detailed list of project deliverables (both interim and finish), a detailed estimate of project tasks, a list of activities and phases, a detailed estimate of the time and resources required to complete all project tasks, and information about the preferences of the project team regarding schedule format.

DEVELOPING A WORKABLE PROJECT SCHEDULE

UNDERSTANDING THE OBJECTIVE

This objective expands on Objective 2.2. After developing a detailed list of project tasks and deliverables, estimated durations, task resources, and preferences on schedule formats, project teams must create a schedule that serves as a guide for completing a project on time.

WHAT YOU REALLY NEED TO KNOW

◆ A good schedule is a key tool for guiding the completion of work. Many people are motivated by deadlines, and seeing their names attached to schedules clarifies accountability and progress. Project managers should work with their teams to create and maintain workable project schedules.

◆ There are several ways to display schedule information. Most schedules list project tasks, deliverables, and completion dates as a minimum.

◆ Many people like to see **milestone reports**, which list project milestones in one column and their planned completion dates in the next column.

◆ The project team often needs more detailed schedule information, such as the resources assigned to specific tasks and the dependencies between tasks. A **Gantt chart** is a popular and effective tool for displaying detailed schedule information. The WBS provides the basis for the list of tasks and their hierarchy. **Project network diagrams** display task dependencies and provide automatic generation of task dates.

◆ By using **project management software** to create Gantt charts and project network diagrams, you can easily create good project schedules and change the format and amount of detail displayed. For example, you can provide reports that list tasks by resource. However, remember the saying, "Garbage in means garbage out." You must have good inputs to create good schedules.

◆ You can also track planned versus actual information as the project progresses, using a **tracking Gantt chart** or similar tool. The project team should decide whether and how it wishes to track actual schedule information.

OBJECTIVES ON THE JOB

Project schedules should guide completion of work. Create and use them with this intent.

PRACTICE TEST QUESTIONS

1. **Which of the following items are needed to create a detailed project schedule? Select three answers.**
   a. a detailed cost estimate
   b. a detailed list of tasks and deliverables
   c. planned start and end dates for tasks
   d. task dependencies
   e. duration estimates for milestones

2. **How can you use a project schedule to motivate people to complete their work? Select two answers.**
   a. List the names of people working on tasks on the project schedule.
   b. List the costs for resources on tasks on the project schedule.
   c. Track planned and actual schedule progress.
   d. Use penalties for any task finished late.

3. **What is the minimum information needed for a project schedule?**
   a. task dependencies
   b. completion dates for tasks and/or deliverables
   c. start dates for tasks and/or deliverables
   d. a list of tasks and/or deliverables

4. **Match the following schedule formats to the people who would most likely prefer them.**

Milestone report	a. Most project stakeholders
Gantt chart	b. Select stakeholders
Network diagram	c. Senior management
Tracking Gantt chart	d. Project manager

5. **Your company uses sophisticated project management software to enter, track, and communicate all types of project information. You have spent a lot of time developing a good baseline plan for your project. You also require your team to enter actuals. It appeared from the software that everything was going fine, but you discovered a lot of schedule-related problems at the last team meeting. How could this happen? Select two answers:**
   a. The software is not working properly.
   b. People are not entering accurate data.
   c. There are personality clashes on the team.
   d. People are not entering timely data.

6. **What is the main purpose of project schedules?**
   a. to meet contractual requirements
   b. to display information in a graphic format
   c. to guide completion of work
   d. to keep management informed

2.13 Given a project planning scenario, demonstrate an understanding of and the ability to plan for iteration by identifying elements likely to require it and explicitly deciding to provide for iteration in the project plan (e.g., scope approval, plan approval, project design, final deliverable turnover, etc.).

PLANNING FOR ITERATION IN PROJECT PLANS

UNDERSTANDING THE OBJECTIVE

Because of the unique nature of projects, plans are expected to become more defined as the project progresses. Project teams should plan for scope documents, design documents, and related information to go through an iterative process of development as detailed plans are set forth.

WHAT YOU REALLY NEED TO KNOW

◆ Projects are unique and temporary by definition. Project plans will become more detailed as time progresses, so it is important to plan for **iteration**.

◆ Time and resources should be allocated to review, analyze, and improve project plans. People on the project team and other stakeholders, especially users of information technology products, should be actively involved in the iterative development of plans.

◆ Items most likely to require careful iteration include scope documents, including definitions of product designs and project deliverables. For example, an original description of a deliverable might be fairly broad. As it comes closer to the time to create or acquire the deliverable, that description must be further elaborated.

◆ Project plans should include a process for submitting preliminary documents, obtaining feedback on them, incorporating feedback, and receiving appropriate approval.

◆ Iteration is also required when planning for turnover of final deliverables. For example, many changes can occur from the time a project begins to the time it ends. Preliminary plans can describe the turnover of final deliverables, but more detailed plans must be provided at the end of the project to ensure a smooth transition.

OBJECTIVES ON THE JOB

Iteration is an important part of project planning. Remember to allocate time and resources for updating plans during the life of the project.

PRACTICE TEST QUESTIONS

1. **Which of the following items are mostly likely to require iterative planning? Select three answers.**
   a. the project scope
   b. design of deliverables
   c. the budgeting process
   d. project quality
   e. the deliverable turnover process

2. **Your project team is rewriting a project scope definition for a systems development project to make requirements clearer. You have invited users of the new system to the meetings, but only a few could attend. How can you make sure the users will be satisfied with the project scope? Select two answers.**
   a. Use teleconferencing to improve user involvement.
   b. Continue to involve users at the iterative planning meetings.
   c. Require a minimum number of users at a meeting for it to continue.
   d. Require user sign-off on important documents.

3. **You are managing a project to produce an information system for a new marketing campaign. Your plans have focused on the need to deliver the system by a specific date, in order for it to be useful. You have just found out the marketing campaign has been postponed for three months. What should you do? Select two answers.**
   a. Discuss the schedule changes at an planning meeting.
   b. Continue the project as scheduled.
   c. Ask the project sponsor and senior management for advice.
   d. Stop working on the project for three months so the system is done on a just-in-time basis.

4. **What steps should be included in the project planning process? Select three answers.**
   a. submitting preliminary plans
   b. obtaining feedback on preliminary plans
   c. entering plans into an automated system
   d. receiving appropriate approval for plans

5. **Your team has just completed an upgrade to an important information system. You delivered everything as scheduled, and the system passed the user acceptance test. At the final project meeting, the functional manager of the information systems group responsible for system maintenance is complaining that he or she does not have staff who know how to maintain some of the new technologies used in the new system. What should you do? Select two answers.**
   a. Document lessons learned, so as to do a better job of transition planning.
   b. Defer to someone else, since you completed your job as project manager.
   c. Outsource the maintenance work to an experienced supplier.
   d. Discuss options for resolving this problem.

OBJECTIVES

2.14 Given a scenario involving tasks, resources (fixed or variable), and dependences for a multiphase IT project, demonstrate knowledge of the standards for creating a workable WBS. Recognize and explain the need to creatively visualize all deliverables (interim and finished) and thoroughly decompose the system into all potential hardware and software components.

CREATING A WBS

UNDERSTANDING THE OBJECTIVE

A work breakdown structure (WBS) is a foundation document in project management. It provides the basis for planning and managing project schedules, costs, and changes. It is crucial to work with the team to create a good WBS.

WHAT YOU REALLY NEED TO KNOW

◆ A **work breakdown structure** is an outcome-oriented analysis of the work involved in a project that defines the total scope of the project (see ITPM2e, p. 100-107).

◆ A WBS should list all the work, and only the work, required to complete the project. It is important to include tasks related to creating the products of the project, as well as the process for developing them. A WBS is required for creating a Gantt chart.

◆ A WBS shows tasks in a **hierarchy** format. Each WBS item is the sum of the WBS items below it. The highest level of the WBS, Level 0, is the entire project. The next level, Level 1, lists major groupings for tasks. The next level breaks down those major groupings into more specific tasks, and the decomposition continues.

◆ The lowest level in a WBS is called a **work package**. Experts suggest that work packages involve no more than eighty hours of work, but there are wide variations in the number of levels and amount of detail in WBSs. The nature of the project should drive the structure of the WBS.

◆ A WBS is often depicted in graphical format as a task-oriented family tree of tasks resembling an organization chart. A WBS can also be displayed in tabular form with a numbering scheme and indentations depicting the hierarchy of tasks. For example, the structure below shows a tabular format for a WBS:

1.0 Main task 1

    1.1 Subtask 1

    1.2 Subtask 2

2.0 Main task 2

3.0 Main task 3

OBJECTIVES ON THE JOB

Work with the project team to create a good WBS. Take the time to do it well.

PRACTICE TEST QUESTIONS

1. **What tool provides the basis for planning and managing project schedules, costs, and changes?**
   a. a responsibility assignment matrix
   b. a resource histogram
   c. a project network diagram
   d. a work breakdown structure

2. **What do you call the lowest level in a WBS?**
   a. a task
   b. a subtask
   c. a work package
   d. a milestone

3. **You are reviewing a draft WBS created by some of your project team. You notice that the WBS is one long list of tasks. What basic principle of WBS creation has your team neglected?**
   a. creating a hierarchy of tasks
   b. showing a WBS in a graphic format
   c. entering the WBS into project management software
   d. including milestones in the WBS

4. **What do you call the level that includes the entire project?**
   a. Level 0
   b. Level 1
   c. Level 2
   d. Level 3

5. **How is a WBS related to a Gantt chart?**
   a. The WBS provides the list of tasks included on a Gantt chart.
   b. Deliverables on a WBS provide the list of tasks on a Gantt chart.
   c. Summary tasks on a WBS provide the list of tasks on a Gantt chart.
   d. You do not need a WBS to create a Gantt chart.

6. **The WBS provides the basis for planning and managing which of the following items on a project? Select three answers.**
   a. schedules
   b. costs
   c. quality
   d. changes

2.15 Recognize and explain the need to obtain consensus among all stakeholders regarding project deliverables and other elements in the WBS, and obtain formal approval (sign-off) of project sponsor(s) regarding project deliverables and other elements of the WBS.

OBTAINING CONSENSUS AND FORMAL APPROVAL OF THE WBS

UNDERSTANDING THE OBJECTIVE

People who will do the work in a project should be involved in planning the work. People who are sponsoring or paying for the work should also have a say in what gets done. Plan to obtain formal approval on project deliverables, especially if you are under contract, which is legally binding.

WHAT YOU REALLY NEED TO KNOW

◆ **Consensus** means reaching agreement on a collective decision. It is very important to involve all affected stakeholders in identifying and describing the deliverables and other parts of a WBS. It often takes several formal and informal meetings and other forms of communication to reach consensus on the project scope.

◆ Each WBS item must be documented to ensure accurate understanding of what is and is not included in that item. Each deliverable should be defined in detail. Information technology deliverables often require detailed specifications. It is important to keep descriptions of WBS items up-to-date as the project progresses.

◆ Clarify who is responsible for performing specific tasks in the WBS. Each WBS item should be the responsibility of only one individual, even though many people may be working on it. If there are problems with a particular WBS item, the appropriate person should be contacted. Bigger problems should be elevated to the person in charge of the aggregated WBS item, and problems related to the entire project should be directed to the project manager.

◆ In order to acknowledge consensus and follow the necessary chain of command, there should be formal approval of project deliverables and other elements of the WBS. Formal approval often occurs via signatures of the project sponsor(s) or appropriate senior managers.

◆ Problems often result when the wrong people authorize work, so it is important to clarify who can sign off on what. As described in Objective 2.1, a responsibility assignment matrix can be used to clarify stakeholder roles on projects.

OBJECTIVES ON THE JOB

Clarify who is responsible for each WBS item and who can provide formal approval of project deliverables.

PRACTICE TEST QUESTIONS

1. **What term is used to described the process of reaching agreement on a collective decision?**
    a. collaboration
    b. cooperation
    c. coordination
    d. consensus

2. **Who should be involved in identifying and describing project deliverables? Select three answers.**
    a. the project sponsor
    b. configuration management specialists
    c. industrial engineering specialists
    d. users of the deliverables

3. **Users are complaining about a report that your project team delivered. The report included the basic information described in the project plan, but the users expected a much longer, more detailed document than they received. What should you do? Select two answers.**
    a. Tell the users that you delivered what was in the plan.
    b. Work with the users and authors of the report to produce a potential solution.
    c. Ask the authors to redo the report so it meets the users' expectations.
    d. Estimate the impact on the project schedule and budget of redoing the report so it meets the users' expectations.

4. **Why would you want to have only one person responsible for each WBS item? Select two answers.**
    a. to avoid confusion on who does what
    b. because WBS items should be broken down so that one person can do the work
    c. to provide clear accountability for work
    d. to determine performance bonuses more easily

5. **What can you do to ensure that planned and completed work meets the needs of project stakeholders? Select two answers.**
    a. Keep key stakeholders involved in defining and approving WBS items.
    b. Assign users to do most of the work defined in the WBS.
    c. Use a pay-for-performance policy.
    d. Require sign-off on project deliverables.

6. **You have discovered that an important piece of hardware required for your project does not meet specifications. A supplier provided the hardware, but the supplier says it has a signature from a company official accepting the delivery. What should you do? Select two answers.**
    a. Check the contract with the supplier to see who had signature authority.
    b. Return the hardware to the supplier and find another source.
    c. Discuss the problem with the supplier and key stakeholders.
    d. Accept the hardware and do the best you can.

OBJECTIVES

2.16 Given a project scenario with many phases and activities, set realistic, measurable milestones, and demonstrate understanding that measurable targets are required in order to determine if the project is proceeding on time and within budget.

SETTING REALISTIC AND MEASURABLE MILESTONES

UNDERSTANDING THE OBJECTIVE

Project managers must keep the big picture in mind when managing projects. Setting realistic milestones and measuring progress on meeting them helps to keep the project on track.

WHAT YOU REALLY NEED TO KNOW

◆ A **milestone** is a significant event on a project. For example, milestones might include awarding a contract to a supplier, completing the analysis phase of a project, freezing code, going live, delivering workstations, completing training, and so on.

◆ By definition, milestones have no duration. They also do not require any resources or expenditures. Milestones are used on schedules to show significant events that are often the result of related work. For example, there might be several WBS items related to training on a project, but the milestones might only state when training activities begin and when they are completed.

◆ Milestones are represented by a black diamond on a Gantt chart. A slipped milestone is representing by a white diamond on a tracking Gantt chart.

◆ Some people use the **SMART** criteria to help define milestones (see ITPM2e, p. 130-131):

- Specific: It is important to define milestones in enough detail to clarify what they mean.

- Measurable: One of the main reasons for using milestones is to measure progress on a project, so milestones must be easy to measure.

- Assignable: Each milestone should be assigned to one person responsible for its completion.

- Realistic: Projects are much more likely to succeed when they have realistic goals. It is important to make sure that milestones make sense and are achievable.

- Time-framed: Since milestones are part of project schedules, they must be assigned a completion date.

OBJECTIVES ON THE JOB

Senior management and other project stakeholders often want to focus on high-level progress on projects. Project teams should develop a list of important events or milestones for their projects, using the SMART criteria. Focusing on meeting milestones can help everyone stay on track.

PRACTICE TEST QUESTIONS

1. **What is the term used to describe a significant event on a project?**
   - a. a kickoff meeting
   - b. a management review
   - c. a milestone
   - d. a deliverable

2. **How long is a typical milestone on an information technology project?**
   - a. milestone length varies depending on the nature of the project
   - b. zero days
   - c. one month
   - d. one reporting cycle

3. **Which of the following items could be a milestone on a software development project? Select two answers.**
   - a. contract awarded
   - b. develop user training guide
   - c. create test plans
   - d. user acceptance testing completed

4. **Which of the following is not an important characteristic of a milestone?**
   - a. Milestones should be specific.
   - b. Milestones should be realistic.
   - c. Milestones should be assignable.
   - d. Milestones should have clear start and end dates.

5. **You are in the middle of an important project review meeting. You notice that the project sponsor seems bored with all the technical detail being discussed. You want to let everyone know that the project is on track. What should you do?**
   - a. Take the time to discuss project milestones and which ones have been completed so far.
   - b. Review the project network diagram to show the big picture of the project.
   - c. Review the responsibility assignment matrix to show progress on the project.
   - d. Take the time to review the earned value chart to show progress on completing milestones.

6. **You are reviewing a tracking Gantt chart for your project. What do the white diamond symbols represent?**
   - a. milestones
   - b. milestones completed ahead of schedule
   - c. slipped milestones
   - d. deliverables

2.17 Given a set of specific milestones and their descriptions, specify entry and exit criteria for each.

SPECIFYING ENTRY AND EXIT CRITERIA FOR MILESTONES

UNDERSTANDING THE OBJECTIVE

You cannot measure progress in meeting milestones if you do not define their entry and exit criteria. These criteria must be clearly defined by all affected stakeholders.

WHAT YOU REALLY NEED TO KNOW

◆ **Milestones** are determined on the basis of a project's related WBS items. Each phase of a project (i.e., analysis, design, implementation) often has milestones associated with it. Milestones can be used to guide the beginning and end of important project phases.

◆ In order to measure progress toward completing milestones, it is important to relate milestones to associated WBS tasks. For example, there may be several tasks for the analysis phase of a project, and a milestone called "analysis completed" could be placed at the end of the analysis tasks.

◆ Milestones can also help make sure the team is ready to progress on specific tasks. For example, a milestone called "funding approved" could be required before entering a new phase of a project.

◆ Milestones can also be set to help ensure specific tasks are progressing as planned. For example, milestones related to developing software might be "completing Module 1," "completing Module 2," and so on.

◆ As changes are made to a project, it is important to change milestones. There may be a need to modify or add additional milestones to meet changes in the business environment, changes in project design or technology, or changes in personnel.

◆ Focusing on milestones helps everyone understand generally what needs to be done when. Senior managers, in particular, like to focus on meeting milestones to make sure the project is on track.

OBJECTIVES ON THE JOB

Clarify entry and exit points for milestones. Use milestones to make sure the project is progressing toward successful completion.

PRACTICE TEST QUESTIONS

1. **Which of the following WBS items could be viewed as entry criteria to a milestone called "training completed"? Select three answers.**
   a. training materials developed
   b. analysis completed
   c. contract awarded
   d. instructors selected
   e. classrooms scheduled

2. **What can you do to ensure a milestone has actually been met?**
   a. Develop and follow the exit criteria for that milestone.
   b. Check the symbol on the Gantt chart.
   c. Develop and follow the entry criteria for that milestone.

3. **What roles can senior managers take on projects to ensure milestones are measurable? Select three answers.**
   a. Require entry criteria.
   b. Require exit criteria.
   c. Require financial criteria.
   d. Require sign-off on milestones.

4. **A milestone on your project was to receive funding for a certain part of it. You did receive some funding, but you don't think it's enough to justify starting the work. What was wrong with the milestone description?**
   a. It was outdated.
   b. The milestone was not tied to related WBS items.
   c. It was not measurable, since it did not specify how much money was required.
   d. It was not realistic.

5. **You are working with your project team to clarify what milestones are needed to help the project progress. Your initial plans only included a few milestones, but you realize that having more will help motivate your team. What should you do?**
   a. Issue a stop-work order until more milestones are defined.
   b. Work with the project team and other stakeholders to define more milestones.
   c. Ask for additional funding to develop more milestones.
   d. Informally identify some milestones to track.

6. **When can you schedule milestones to help measure progress on important project phases? Select three answers.**
   a. before a phase begins
   b. at incremental points during the phase
   c. at the end of a phase
   d. halfway through the phase, based on the duration of the phase

2.18 Recognize and explain the issues that must be considered in creating a project cost estimate, including project scope, various levels, task requirements, resource skill levels, resource availability, resource expense, and the need to target elapsed time to reconcile the original budget allocation.

RECOGNIZING ISSUES TO CONSIDER IN CREATING A PROJECT COST ESTIMATE

UNDERSTANDING THE OBJECTIVE

You must consider many factors in developing project cost estimates. It is important to understand the nature of the project, organization, and team in order to develop and document realistic assumptions needed to estimate project costs.

WHAT YOU REALLY NEED TO KNOW

◆ There are many issues to consider when creating a project cost estimate:

- Project scope: As previously discussed, it can be very difficult to nail down the scope of a project. Costs are directly related to how much work will be done on a project. The WBS should provide the basis for estimating project costs.

- Task requirements: It is important to understand specific requirements for tasks in order to estimate their costs.

- Resource skill levels: You must consider who will do the work when estimating costs. For example, a senior programmer may do some work more quickly than a junior programmer. The skill level of resources determines the duration estimates for tasks as well as the hourly rates to charge to those tasks.

- Resource availability: If you know the resources that will be on the project, you can create a better estimate. If you want certain resources on the project but they are unavailable, you must take that information into account. You might want to change the schedule to accommodate the availability of resources.

- Resource expense: People are the main resource on projects, and costs for human resources are normally based on hourly rates. These rates include compensation, benefits, overhead, and so on. If resources will be outsourced, you must consider the supplier's costs in creating the cost estimates.

- Original budget allocation: It is very important to keep the budget up-to-date so that everyone is on track. If the original cost estimates are not close to the actuals, you should renegotiate the budget. You must also consider the budget allocation when making initial and revised cost estimates. Scope the work to match the budget.

OBJECTIVES ON THE JOB

Be sure to address factors that affect the project budget throughout the life of the project.

PRACTICE TEST QUESTIONS

1. **Which of the following issues should you consider when creating a project cost estimate? Select three answers.**
   a. project scope
   b. task sequencing
   c. task requirements
   d. resource availability

2. **Why would you want to have a WBS for a project when creating a cost estimate? Select two answers.**
   a. The WBS should provide the basis for estimating project costs.
   b. The WBS provides the numbering scheme needed for the accounting department.
   c. The WBS lists the number of hours people will work on a project.
   d. The WBS shows the scope of work required for a project, which directly affects the costs.

3. **You are estimating the costs for a large information technology project. You discover that your team will consist mostly of junior employees. How will this information affect your cost estimate? Select two answers.**
   a. Your estimated hourly rate will probably be lower than average.
   b. Your estimated durations for tasks will probably be lower than average.
   c. Your estimated hourly rate will probably be higher than average.
   d. Your estimated durations for tasks will probably be higher than average.

4. **You are doing detailed planning for a project, and you discover that a key staff member is unavailable in the month when you really need his/her skills. What should you do?**
   a. Increase the cost estimate to allow for the person to work overtime that month.
   b. Increase the cost estimate to allow for outsourcing of that task.
   c. See if you can adjust the schedule around this person's availability.
   d. Decrease the estimate for that task, since a junior person will have to do it.

5. **How do labor rates of outsourced tasks normally compare to those of in-house tasks?**
   a. They are usually higher.
   b. They are usually lower.
   c. They are about the same.

6. **You have finished the initial planning for a project. Senior management has just cut your budget by thirty percent. What should you do?**
   a. Ask your staff to work more hours without pay.
   b. Reduce the quality of the work accordingly.
   c. Only do the first seventy percent of the project, then ask for additional funds.
   d. Adjust the scope-of-work to match the budget.

OBJECTIVES

2.19 Recognize and explain the issues that must be considered in creating a project time estimate, including project scope, various levels, task requirements, resource skill levels, resource availability, resource expense, and the need to reconcile with the original elapsed time estimation.

RECOGNIZING ISSUES TO CONSIDER IN CREATING A PROJECT TIME ESTIMATE

UNDERSTANDING THE OBJECTIVE

You must consider many factors in developing project time estimates. The issues related to developing project cost estimates are very similar to those for project time estimates. You must understand the nature of the project, organization, and team in order to develop and document realistic assumptions needed to prepare realist time estimates.

WHAT YOU REALLY NEED TO KNOW

◆ There are many issues to consider when creating a project time estimate:

- Project scope: As previously discussed, it can be very difficult to nail down the scope of a project. Time estimates are directly related to how much work will be done on a project. The WBS and resource allocations provide the basis for preparing project time estimates.

- Task requirements: It is important to understand specific requirements for tasks in order to estimate how long it will take to do them. Recall that task durations include the amount of time actually spent performing the work plus elapsed time. There is normally some slack time where resources are not working directly on the project, but those resources are still on the payroll.

- Resource skill levels: You must consider who will do the work when estimating durations. You must also estimate the amount of elapsed time for each task.

- Resource availability: Just as resources drive cost estimates, they also drive schedule estimates. Some tasks require specific resources, so you may need to change the schedule to address the availability of resources.

- Resource expense: Time estimates for human resources are normally based on hours. You should not assume that people are productive 100% of the time, however. Many people assume about 75% productivity, meaning a task that is estimated at twelve hours would be allocated sixteen hours. You must also consider overtime and slack time in preparing time and cost estimates.

- Original elapsed time estimation: It is very important to keep the schedule up-to-date so that everyone stays on track. If the original time estimates are not close to the actuals, you should renegotiate the schedule. Also be aware of techniques to compress schedules, such as fast-tracking and crashing (see ITPM2e, p. 135-136).

OBJECTIVES ON THE JOB

Be sure to address factors that affect the project schedule throughout the life of the project.

PRACTICE TEST QUESTIONS

1. **Which of the following issues should you consider when creating a project schedule? Select three answers.**
   a. resource labor rates
   b. task sequencing
   c. task requirements
   d. resource availability

2. **Why would you want to have a WBS for a project when creating a project schedule? Select two answers.**
   a. The WBS should provide the basis for preparing project time estimates.
   b. The WBS provides the numbering scheme needed for the accounting department.
   c. The WBS lists the number of hours people will work on a project.
   d. The WBS shows the scope-of-work required for the project, which directly affects the schedule.

3. **Your team estimates that they will need to wait two weeks to get user feedback on an important design task. What do you call this time?**
   a. wait time
   b. overhead
   c. slack time
   d. elapsed time

4. **You are preparing a draft schedule for a large information technology project. You discover that your team will consist mostly of junior employees. How will this information affect your time estimates? Select two answers.**
   a. Your estimated number of hours will probably be lower than average.
   b. Your estimated number of dependencies will increase.
   c. Your estimated number of hours will probably be higher than average.
   d. Your estimated elapsed time will be unchanged.

5. **You have finished the initial schedule for a project. Senior management has cut the amount of time you have to complete the project in half. What should you do?**
   a. Ask your staff to work more hours.
   b. Reduce the quality of the work accordingly.
   c. Do only the first half of the project, then ask for additional time and money.
   d. Try to use schedule compression techniques such as fast-tracking and crashing to reduce the schedule.

6. **You are in the early stages of project execution, and it is clear to you that there is no way you can meet the original estimated completion date. What should you do? Select two answers.**
   a. Continue the project as planned.
   b. Inform the project sponsor that you need to renegotiate the schedule.
   c. Develop a new schedule estimate with your project team.
   d. Spend more money to meet the schedule date.

OBJECTIVES

2.20 Recognize and explain the issues that must be considered in creating an effort estimation (man hours, FTEs), including project scope, various levels, task requirements, resource skill levels, resource availability, resource expense, and the need to reconcile with the original staffing allocation.

RECOGNIZING ISSUES TO CONSIDER IN CREATING AN EFFORT ESTIMATION

UNDERSTANDING THE OBJECTIVE

You must consider many issues when developing an estimate of the number of labor hours and/or staff required to complete a project. It is important to consider the context of the project, organization, and resources in preparing effort estimates.

WHAT YOU REALLY NEED TO KNOW

◆ The amount of effort required to complete projects is normally done in terms of labor hours (or person hours) and **full-time equivalent staff (or FTE).**

◆ There are many issues to consider when creating an effort estimation:

- Project scope: Effort estimates are directly related to the project scope. You must know what work is to be done by whom when estimating labor hours or FTE.

- Task requirements: It is important to understand specific requirements for tasks in order to estimate how long it will take to do them.

- Resource skill levels: You must consider who will do the work when estimating labor hours and FTE. Junior employees often require more time to complete tasks. You must also determine whether work will be done in-house or outsourced. If work is outsourced, the in-house hours for administration may need to be increased to oversee the supplier's work.

- Resource availability: Just as resources drive cost and schedule estimates, they also drive effort estimates. You may only need one FTE of a senior employee instead of two for junior employees.

- Resource expense: You must consider the overall project budget when preparing effort estimates. Although you may prefer to use all experienced staff and external suppliers, you may be able to reduce expenses by using more junior staff and doing more work in-house. Likewise, you may think it's better to work in-house when it is actually more economical to outsource the work.

- Original staffing allocation: Project plans should include staffing requirements. If your effort estimates vary from what has been planned, you must coordinate with human resources, functional managers, and other affected stakeholders.

OBJECTIVES ON THE JOB

Be sure to address factors that affect the effort estimates throughout the life of the project.

PRACTICE TEST QUESTIONS

1. **Which of the following issues should you consider when creating a project effort estimate? Select three answers.**
   a. project scope
   b. task sequencing
   c. task requirements
   d. resource availability

2. **You are reviewing an estimate from one of the functional managers supporting your project. Instead of providing labor hours, the estimate mentions FTE. What does FTE stand for?**
   a. functional technical estimate
   b. functional technical expert
   c. full-time equivalent
   d. full-time expert

3. **One of your senior technical people provided an estimate of the number of labor hours required to program a complicated part of your system. What information do you need in order to determine whether or not this estimate is realistic? Select two answers.**
   a. the assumed skill level of the person doing the work
   b. whether the work will be outsourced or not
   c. the assumed programming language used for the estimate
   d. the detailed tasks included in the work

4. **You are at the midpoint of your project schedule, and you have completed the amount of work you had planned. The number of labor hours expended is much higher than planned, but you are still within budget. What are the most likely reasons for this situation? Select two answers.**
   a. Your effort estimates assumed a higher hourly rate.
   b. You outsourced a large part of the work.
   c. You provided a lower level of quality to meet time and cost constraints.
   d. Your project team worked overtime at no additional cost.

5. **You have estimated the effort for your project in FTE. All human resources have been assigned for this totally in-house effort. Your organization's accounting department wants you to translate this information into dollars. What should you do?**
   a. Multiply the FTE for each department by the average cost per FTE.
   b. Ask each person on your team what his/her salary is to provide the estimate.
   c. Ask the human resources department to assist you in providing the necessary information.
   d. Tell the accounting department to figure out the numbers themselves.

OBJECTIVES

2.21 Given a scenario involving project information, including timing, demonstrate the ability to clearly identify what needs to be communicated during a project, to whom, when, how (formal, informal), without creating unnecessary turmoil in the project team, in situations such as schedule changes, resource loss, personality clashes, budget changes, low morale, organizational changes, and project phase completion.

COMMUNICATING IN STRESSFUL SITUATIONS

UNDERSTANDING THE OBJECTIVE

Good communications are crucial for project success, especially in stressful situations. Projects should have a communications plan for predictable situations, but project managers should also be prepared to communicate difficult information.

WHAT YOU REALLY NEED TO KNOW

◆ Even when things go well, it is difficult to communicate project information. When things don't go so well, it is even more difficult to communicate necessary information.

◆ Project managers should strive to provide good communications without creating unnecessary turmoil in the project team. It is usually better to be honest and timely in communicating potentially disruptive information.

◆ Typical problems that may surface on projects include the following:

- Schedule, budget, and organizational changes: Because projects work in the broader context of organizations, they are subject to changes in the organization. If the project manager learns of potential changes to the project that may affect the schedule or budget, he/she should communicate the information as clearly as possible to affected stakeholders. It is also important to communicate organizational changes such as restructuring, that may affect the project.

- Resource loss: If a key project team member quits or is fired, it is best to communicate the information directly to the project team. Withholding information often results in confusion, rumors, and a reduction in team productivity.

- Personality clashes: Emotional conflict on projects hurts productivity. The project manager should set ground rules for team behavior to minimize this problem. In the event that individuals simply cannot work together, the project manager should consider reassignment.

- Low morale: There are many causes of low morale. The project manager should make sure the project is important to the organization, well defined, and well managed to avoid low morale.

OBJECTIVES ON THE JOB

Project communications are even more important during stressful situations. Be open and honest.

PRACTICE TEST QUESTIONS

1. **Which of the following are potential causes of stress on projects? Select three answers.**
   a. loss of resources
   b. schedule changes
   c. low morale
   d. communications requirements

2. **Two members of your project team have frequent arguments. It is clear that they cannot work together. What should you do?**
   a. Relocate their desks to minimize face-to-face contact.
   b. Publicly state that you will not tolerate such childish behavior.
   c. Reassign one of the individuals.
   d. Relocate their desk right next to each other to force them to work things out.

3. **You heard rumors that your company is being bought and that all information technology work will be the responsibility of the new company. You have a project status meeting the next day. What should you tell your project team, which has been working hard on an important information technology project?**
   a. nothing
   b. everything
   c. to ignore rumors and that you will find out what is really happening
   d. to look for a new job

4. **An important project stakeholder on your project is leaving your company. He/she sent an e-mail to all employees stating how glad he/she was to leave because the company was going down the drain. What should you do?**
   a. Reply to the e-mail and wish the person well.
   b. Reply to the e-mail and say how great your current company is.
   c. Do not reply to the e-mail, but address the situation at a project team meeting.
   d. Contact the stakeholder's new employer and tell them not to hire this person.

5. **You are in the middle of an important project review meeting. Someone walks in and states that the project sponsor has just died from a heart attack. What should you do?**
   a. Continue the meeting as planned.
   b. Allow people to express their concerns, then reschedule the meeting.
   c. Issue a stop-work order on the project.
   d. Reprimand the person for interrupting your meeting.

6. **You have to lay off three people on your project team. Which communications approach is most appropriate?**
   a. Meet individually, face-to-face, with each person.
   b. Call all three people into your office to let them know together.
   c. Send a sealed letter to each individual affected.
   d. Call each person at home later that evening to let him/her know.

OBJECTIVES

2.22 Identify the components of an adequate project plan and explain the function of each. Components include a table of contents, overview, sponsors, team members, requirements, scheduled tasks (WBS), expected resources, environmental issues, business requirements, implementation plans, support plans, and training plans.

ORGANIZING A COMPREHENSIVE PROJECT PLAN

UNDERSTANDING THE OBJECTIVE

It is much easier to execute a project when there is a comprehensive project plan. It is important to understand the contents of a project plan and to create a good one to guide project execution.

WHAT YOU REALLY NEED TO KNOW

◆ Project plans vary with the needs of a project. General components include the following:

- Table of contents: Project plans can be lengthy documents, so it is important to include a table of contents up front.

- Overview: An overview or executive summary is often included at the beginning of project plan to provide a big-picture perspective on the project.

- Sponsors and team members: The project plan should clearly identify the key stakeholders, especially the sponsors and project team. Individual names and contact information should be included.

- Requirements: A large part of project plans is often related to requirements. The project plan should include a WBS, descriptions of WBS items, product specifications, business and technical requirements, and so on.

- Expected resources: Project plans should include staffing information and relevant resource information.

- Environmental issues: Because projects work in a broader organizational context, the project plan should include issues related to the environment.

- Implementation plans: Many information technology projects require detailed implementation plans as part of the project plans. For example, if a project includes installing hardware and software in different locations, the implementation plan would describe these installations.

- Support plans and training plans: The project plan should also include information related to supporting project deliverables and training people in using any new hardware or software resulting from the project.

OBJECTIVES ON THE JOB

Review potential contents of a project plan. Be sure your project has a good plan to make execution run more smoothly.

PRACTICE TEST QUESTIONS

1. **Which of the following are normally components of a project plan? Select three answers.**
   a. support plans
   b. training plans
   c. senior management biographies
   d. expected resources

2. **Which part of a project plan provides a summary of the project?**
   a. the table of contents
   b. the project charter
   c. the overview section
   d. the requirements section

3. **You are planning a large information technology project that involves delivering thousands of computers to several locations. Which part of the project plan should describe these deliveries?**
   a. the implementation plan
   b. the execution plan
   c. the installation plan
   d. the integration plan

4. **Why should the project plan include the names and contact information for the project team and sponsor? Select two answers.**
   a. to help communications
   b. for legal reasons
   c. to promote accountability and buy-in
   d. to inform people that they are assigned to a project

5. **You are taking over the role of project manager on a multimillion-dollar project. Your sponsor wants you to quickly begin executing the project, but there is no real project plan. What should you do? Select two answers.**
   a. Do as the sponsor asks and begin project execution.
   b. Explain to the sponsor that execution will go much more smoothly after you have a good project plan.
   c. Meet with the project team and work hard to develop a good project plan quickly.
   d. Use a template for a past project as your project plan.

6. **What topic often takes up a lot of room in a project plan for an information technology project?**
   a. the overview
   b. resource information
   c. requirements information
   d. budget information

2.23 Identify the steps involved in organizing a comprehensive project plan and using it to close out the planning phase of a project. Steps include assembling all project planning elements, creating an outline or table of contents, reviewing the outline with the project sponsor and key stakeholders, writing the comprehensive project plan, circulating the plan, obtaining top management support, conducting a formal review, adjusting the plan, and obtaining formal approval of the project plan.

IDENTIFYING THE STEPS IN ORGANIZING A COMPREHENSIVE PROJECT PLAN AND USING IT TO CLOSE OUT THE PLANNING PHASE

UNDERSTANDING THE OBJECTIVE

It is crucial to involve key project stakeholders in creating the project plan. Allow for time to receive input from stakeholders, gain top-management support for the project, review the plan, make changes, and obtain formal approval.

WHAT YOU REALLY NEED TO KNOW

◆ People who will do the work should be heavily involved in planning the work. A project is much more likely to succeed if careful thought is put into planning and the right people are involved in developing the project plan.

◆ It is also crucial to have people who will review or receive the products of the project involved in the planning process. There are often many things that are subject to interpretation, so use an iterative planning process.

◆ Steps in developing and receiving approval on a project plan include the following:

- Assembling all project planning elements: Be sure to identify relevant parts of a project plan that are applicable to your particular project.

- Creating an outline and reviewing it with key stakeholders: Involve key stakeholders early in the planning process. An outline helps to make sure everyone is on the same page in terms of what should be in the plan. Reviewing similar plans or templates for project plans can help.

- Writing the comprehensive project plan: The full plan often includes many pages of information, graphics, exhibits, and appendices.

- Circulating the plan to all stakeholders and obtaining top-management support: To obtain buy-in and commitment, be sure to send a good draft of the plan to all stakeholders, including relevant senior management.

- Conducting a formal review, adjusting the plan, and obtaining formal approval. The project team should incorporate feedback and hold a formal review meeting. Further adjustments may be made at or after the meeting. Then the project sponsor should formally sign off on the plan.

OBJECTIVES ON THE JOB

Follow a good process for developing and receiving approval on a project plan.

PRACTICE TEST QUESTIONS

1. **Put the following steps for creating a project plan in sequence.**
   a. Adjust the comprehensive plan on the basis of stakeholder feedback.
   b. Assemble all project planning elements.
   c. Create an outline or table of contents.
   d. Review the outline with key stakeholders.
   e. Write the comprehensive project plan.
   f. Obtain formal approval.

2. **Which of the following are steps involved in organizing a comprehensive project plan? Select three answers.**
   a. Adjust the comprehensive plan on the basis of stakeholder feedback.
   b. Assemble all project planning elements.
   c. Enter the plan into corporate project management software.
   d. Review the outline with key stakeholders.

3. **Why should you obtain feedback on a table of contents for a project plan? Select two answers.**
   a. to make sure the necessary components are included in the plan
   b. to avoid litigation
   c. to spread the workload
   d. to create buy-in

4. **How can you make sure that a project plan has top-management support? Select two answers.**
   a. Require a senior manager to provide introductory comments at important project meetings.
   b. Make sure the plan reflects senior management concerns.
   c. Require a senior manager to edit the plan.
   d. Provide an opportunity for senior management to provide input.

5. **You are new to project management and have been asked to lead your team in developing a comprehensive project plan. How should you proceed? Select three answers.**
   a. Find samples of project plans for similar projects.
   b. Find templates for developing project plans.
   c. Hire an outside consultant to develop the plan.
   d. Ask your project team and other stakeholders for help in getting started.

6. **You have sent a detailed outline of your project plan out for review, but not a single stakeholder has provided any feedback What should you do? Select two answers.**
   a. Personally contact key stakeholders and stress the importance of getting their feedback early in the planning process.
   b. Send an e-mail reminding everyone that comments are due by a specific date and that you cannot accept late feedback.
   c. Ask a senior manager to issue a memo requiring feedback by a certain date.
   d. Hold a short meeting to review the outline and get feedback.

Domain III

OBJECTIVES

3.1 Identify tasks that should be accomplished on a weekly basis in the course of tracking an "up and running" project.

IDENTIFYING TASKS FOR TRACKING PROJECTS

UNDERSTANDING THE OBJECTIVE

While projects are active or "up and running," there are many tasks to do to make sure projects are on track. It is important to decide which tasks to do and how to adapt them to different situations.

WHAT YOU REALLY NEED TO KNOW

◆ Weekly tasks in tracking active projects include:

- Checking the project's scope status to determine whether project elements are "in-scope" or "out-of-scope." Since it is easy for scope creep to occur, it is important to verify that work being planned and accomplished is within the scope of the project.

- Checking the evolution and status of project deliverables. Stakeholders expect projects to deliver products and services, so it is important to ensure deliverables are on track.

- Check the project schedule. As projects progress, it is essential to check current versus planned schedule progress. If schedules need to change, the project team should work with key stakeholders to negotiate a workable schedule.

- Analyze variances by comparing "estimated" to "actual" resource time expenditures, dollar expenditures, and elapsed duration of activities. A **variance** is a deviation from plan. For example, if the plan was to take one week to complete a tasks and it ends up taking two weeks, there is a one-week variance.

- Handle scope changes, if needed. It is very important to address requests for change to the project scope and handle them wisely.

- List, track, and try to resolve open issues. Open and up-to-date communications are crucial. Many project teams find that issue tracking improves project communications.

- Report project status. To keep stakeholders apprised of how the project is going, project managers should prepare some type of weekly status report.

- Look for opportunities to "push" for close-out of activities and sign-off of deliverables. Project managers must continually strive for successful completion of projects. Activities and deliverables must be closed out in a timely manner.

- Decide whether it's necessary to kill the project, then do so if appropriate. It is very difficult for people to admit failure, but there are several good reasons for terminating or killing projects. If a project is not meeting organizational needs, it is important for project managers and senior management to end or redirect the effort.

OBJECTIVES ON THE JOB

Perform tasks that are necessary to track project progress. Continue to focus on organizational needs.

PRACTICE TEST QUESTIONS

1. **Which of the following tasks should be accomplished on a weekly basis to keep track of current projects? Select three answers.**
   a. Check the project schedule.
   b. Decide if it's necessary to kill the project.
   c. Decide if the current project manager should continue.
   d. List, track, and try to resolve open issues.
   e. Suggest scope changes.

2. **What is a variance?**
   a. a buffer in a duration estimate
   b. a small amount of money set aside for contingencies
   c. a form of risk management
   d. deviation from the project plan

3. **Your project sponsor insists on weekly project status reports, including an assessment of whether it's necessary to kill the project. You think it's unnecessary and unproductive to address the possibility of killing the project. Which of the follow situations would merit a weekly report on project viability? Select two answers.**
   a. The organizations is under severe financial distress.
   b. The project sponsor does not trust the project manager.
   c. There is a parallel project that will also meet business needs.
   d. The CEO is nearing retirement.

4. **Your project team has a difficult time letting go of completed tasks and moving on to new tasks on your project. What can you do to help this situation? Select two answers.**
   a. Require weekly issue tracking.
   b. Push for close out of activities.
   c. Get sign-off on deliverables.
   d. Require checks on the project's scope status.

5. **Several of the technical people working on your project complain about submitting weekly project status information. A few of them simply do not submit required reports. What should you do to change this undesired behavior? Select two answers.**
   a. Reward team members who do submit timely reports.
   b. Leave the technical workers alone so they can do more important work.
   c. Assign someone else to submit the status reports.
   d. Issue a minor punishment for not submitting reports.

6. **You are in the early stages of project execution. Why should you emphasize the need for team members to check the project's scope status when you just completed defining the scope? Select two answers.**
   a. You want to avoid scope creep.
   b. Your team did not do a good job of defining the scope.
   c. You want to ensure that the work being accomplished is what was planned.
   d. Your project sponsor is a very important person in the organization.

OBJECTIVES

3.2   Given an approved project and a significant budget increase in one area of the project, clearly identify the reason for and the size of the increase, identify options for absorbing part or all of the increase in the overall budget, and identify stakeholders that must be notified or give approval and develop a plan for advising them of the change.

HANDLING BUDGET INCREASES

UNDERSTANDING THE OBJECTIVE

Sometimes projects are approved with a minimum amount of funds. Organizations may then increase the budget for various reasons, such as to fund overtime or to purchase items that were more expensive than anticipated. Project managers must handle these budget increases in a professional manner.

WHAT YOU REALLY NEED TO KNOW

◆ There are several reasons for project budgets to increase, such as the following:
- Estimates for labor may have been low.
- Personnel may be required to work overtime to meet deadlines.
- Estimates for materials may have been low.
- There might be an opportunity to increase quality by spending more on labor or materials.
- The customer might increase the scope of the project.

◆ The project manager should clearly identify the reason for the budget increase and the size of the increase, and use the funds accordingly.

◆ If additional funds are not assigned to specific tasks, the project team must work with key stakeholders to determine the best way to use the budget increase. The person providing the additional funds should have a large say in how the money is used.

◆ The project manager should inform affected stakeholders about the budget increase. The rationale for the increase should be clearly communicated.

OBJECTIVES ON THE JOB

Project teams should be happy to receive an increase in funds for a project. It is important to use the funds wisely.

PRACTICE TEST QUESTIONS

1. **Which of the following reasons might cause an increase in funding for a project? Select three answers.**
   a. The accounting department misreported budget information.
   b. The organization received a tax rebate.
   c. The project team needs to work extra hours to complete the project on time.
   d. The customer wants to purchase more expensive materials than planned.
   e. Labor rates were higher than planned.

2. **What should a project manager do if the budget for a project is increased? Select three answers.**
   a. Determine the reason for the increase.
   b. Determine the size of the increase.
   c. Allocate the increase uniformly across the project.
   d. Notify stakeholders of the increase use the funds for contingencies.

3. **You have just finished detailed planning for a large information technology project. Your team is starting to execute the plan when your sponsor notifies you that he/she wants to double the project budget. What should you do?**
   a. Hold a celebration party for all project stakeholders, using some of the funds.
   b. Clarify the reason for the increase, then use the money accordingly.
   c. Work with your project team leaders to decide how best to use the money.
   d. Give personnel a raise and order higher quality materials for the project.

4. **Your project team is halfway through the execution phase of a large development project. You project that you cannot finish this important project on time unless your staff is paid to work 20% overtime for the next two months. What should you do? Select two answers.**
   a. Discuss the situation with the project sponsor and request additional funds.
   b. Reduce the amount of money you are spending on a vendor to get the overtime funds.
   c. Spend the overtime and ask for additional funds later in the project.
   d. Prepare a detailed estimate of the additional funds required.

5. **You have just started executing a project for your organization when the project sponsor notifies you that he/she wants to double the project budget. Who should be involved in deciding how to use the additional funds? Select three answers.**
   a. the project sponsor
   b. vendors working on the project
   c. the project manager
   d. the project team

OBJECTIVES

3.3 Given a scenario in which a vendor requests a two week delay in delivering its product, explain how to negotiate a lesser delay by identifying things the vendor might do to improve its schedule, clearly identify the impact of the negotiated delivery on the project scope, and present this impact to the appropriate stakeholders.

ADDRESSING VENDOR DELAYS

UNDERSTANDING THE OBJECTIVE

Many information technology projects involve vendors or suppliers to provide goods and services required for the project. It is important to manage vendor relationships well, even when vendors cannot deliver as planned.

WHAT YOU REALLY NEED TO KNOW

◆ Vendors provide goods and services for many information technology projects. Vendors plan their activities and schedules, but sometimes they have difficulty executing their plans.

◆ Changes to delivery dates from vendors often impact other project tasks. If a vendor asks for a two-week delay in delivering a product, the project team must assess the affect of this delay. If the delivery is not on the critical path of the project and has two weeks' slack, there should not be any impact. However, there is rarely that much slack provided for deliverables.

◆ If a vendor requests an extension in providing deliverables, the project manager should first see if there is a possibility of negotiating a shorter delay. There might be things the vendor could do to improve the schedule, such as working overtime or assigning a higher priority to this project.

◆ The project manager should also review the contract with the vendor to see if there are penalties for late delivery. Reminding vendors of late penalties could motivate them to deliver the product on time. The project manager could also consider providing a financial incentive for meeting or beating future delivery dates.

◆ If it is determined that there will be a delay of deliverables, the project manager and team should clearly identify the effect on the project scope, time, and cost and inform all affected stakeholders as soon as possible.

OBJECTIVES ON THE JOB

Develop good relationships with vendors and work with them to meet delivery dates. If vendor products are delayed, determine the impact on the project as quickly as possible and communicate necessary information to affected stakeholders.

PRACTICE TEST QUESTIONS

1. **Which of the following would be legitimate reasons for a vendor to request a delay in delivering a product? Select two answers.**
   a. The vendor may have underestimated the amount of time required to produce and deliver the product.
   b. The project contact from the vendor's organization may be going on vacation.
   c. The vendor might be able to provide a better product by delivering the product late.
   d. The vendor might lose money by delivering the product late.

2. **A vendor has just requested a two-week extension in delivering a product for your project, but he/she insists it will not affect the overall schedule. How could this statement be true? Select two answers.**
   a. The product might not be an important one for the project.
   b. Delivery of the product is on the critical path.
   c. Delivery of the product is not on the critical path.
   d. There are two weeks of slack for delivering the product.

3. **A vendor requests a delay in delivering an important product for your project. What should you do? Select two answers.**
   a. Try to negotiate a lesser delay.
   b. Work with the vendor to try to improve its schedule.
   c. Enforce a fine for late delivery of the product.
   d. Try to find a different vendor to deliver the product.

4. **A vendor requests a delay in delivering an important product for your project. How can you shorten the delay in delivery of a vendor product?**
   a. Suggest the vendor's staff work overtime.
   b. Suggest the vendor provide a product of lower quality.
   c. Ask the vendor to give this product a low priority.
   d. Ask the vendor to double spending on the product.

5. **A vendor delay will affect several other tasks on the critical path of your project. What should you do? Select two answers.**
   a. Meet with affected stakeholders to discuss options for staying on schedule.
   b. Meet with affected stakeholders to discuss options for minimizing schedule impacts.
   c. Meet with senior management to discuss how to handle this problem.
   d. Inform the vendor's senior management that you will not do further business with them.

6. **When should you inform affected stakeholders of an important schedule delay?**
   a. when the delay actually occurs
   b. as soon as possible
   c. at the next status review meeting

OBJECTIVES

3.4 Given a scenario in which there is a disagreement between a vendor and your project team, identify methods for resolving the problem.

RESOLVING PROBLEMS WITH VENDORS

UNDERSTANDING THE OBJECTIVE

It is important to develop and sustain good relationships with vendors. When problems arise, project teams should understand and use appropriate conflict resolution strategies.

WHAT YOU REALLY NEED TO KNOW

◆ Many information technology projects involve acquiring goods and/or services from vendors. Try to prevent and watch for common problems, especially in the following areas:

- Vendors may not meet delivery dates. It is important to make delivery dates clear, check on the status of deliverables, and write contracts to motivate vendors to deliver on time.

- Vendors may not provide the level of quality expected. Contracts with vendors should specify the quality of deliverables. It is also important for the project team to work closely with vendors to ensure quality.

- Vendors may try to increase prices for goods and services. Vendors may bid low and then expect add-on work to make more money. Be careful to write contracts carefully and monitor vendor work. Also check references and past performance of vendors.

- Vendors may not be objective in making recommendations for products. Don't expect a hardware vendor to recommend a competing company's hardware. Be careful in selecting the proper vendors for goods and services.

◆ Should problems arise between vendors and your project team, use good conflict management.

◆ As mentioned in Objective 2.6, there are several conflict handling modes. Try to use the confrontation or problem-solving mode to resolve conflicts. Also remember that task-related conflict is often good for projects, especially when it helps the team brainstorm new ideas and find better ways to resolve problems.

OBJECTIVES ON THE JOB

Realize that it is natural for people to have disagreements, especially when they work for different companies. Try to prevent common problems with vendors and manage them wisely when they do occur.

PRACTICE TEST QUESTIONS

1. **Which of the following are common problems with vendors on information technology project? Select three answers.**
    a. Vendors may be late with deliverables.
    b. The project team and vendors may have diversity problems.
    c. Vendors may have different views of quality.
    d. Vendors may not make objective recommendations.

2. **You know that vendors have a tendency to try to increase prices for goods and services after they are under contract. What can you do to prevent this problem from happening? Select three answers.**
    a. Use only fixed price contracts.
    b. Monitor vendor work.
    c. Write contracts carefully.
    d. Check references and past performance of vendors.

3. **You are working with a vendor to determine the best software package for your organization to buy. Several of your project team members strongly disagree with the vendor's recommendations, mainly because the vendor recommends only its own products. How should you proceed?**
    a. Have an impartial party review and analyze potential software packages from several vendors.
    b. Discuss the problem with the vendor and ask for his/her suggestions.
    c. Try to get a special deal for selecting the vendor's software.
    d. Elevate the problem to senior management.

4. **Which conflict handling mode is normally the best to use for resolving problems with vendors?**
    a. confrontation
    b. compromise
    c. smoothing
    d. forcing

5. **You believe that vendors have a tendency to deliver goods and services late. What strategies can you use to prevent late deliveries? Select two answers.**
    a. Include late penalties in the contract.
    b. Add extra time in the project schedule for all vendor deliverables.
    c. Include financial incentives for early or on-time deliveries.
    d. Plan for a back-up vendor for most deliverables.

6. **Members of your project team disagree with the vendor's technical approach to a task on a software development project. What should you do?**
    a. Tell the vendor that you agree with your team's approach.
    b. Tell your team that you agree with the vendor's approach.
    c. Suggest everyone brainstorm potential solutions.
    d. Tell everyone to stop arguing over tasks because it will hurt project performance.

OBJECTIVES

3.5   Identify issues to consider when trying to rebuild active project support from a wavering executive (e.g., the need to identify the source of doubts, interpersonal communications skills that might be employed, the need to act without creating negative impact, the need to identify and utilize various allies and influences, etc.). Given a scenario involving a wavering executive, choose an appropriate course of action.

REBUILDING ACTIVE SUPPORT FROM A WAVERING EXECUTIVE

UNDERSTANDING THE OBJECTIVE

An important factor related to success on information technology projects is executive support. If an executive is wavering on support of your project, identify the reason for the change in behavior and try to rebuild support.

WHAT YOU REALLY NEED TO KNOW

◆ Projects normally have executive support when they are initiated, but that support may subside as the project progresses.

◆ Project managers and their teams often need executive support during crucial times of execution. Important decisions must be made that may impact many aspects of a company. It is important to maintain executive support for the project as it progresses.

◆ In a situation where an important executive is wavering in support of the project:

- Identify the source of doubts. Find out why the executive is not as supportive. Ask the executive directly what is happening. If that approach does not work, talk to other people who might know what the problem is.

- Use interpersonal communication skills. Only 7% of communications are the actual words that people use. Project managers should know how to read body language and interpret voice tones so that they understand how people are really feeling during a discussion. Face-to-face communications are crucial so that the project manager can get to the heart of the problem when an executive is wavering on support.

- Acting without creating negative impact. Project managers must be sensitive to needs of the organization. What is in the best interest of one particular project may not be best for the entire organization. Executives may waver on support of a project because there are more important issues to consider.

- Identify and use allies and influences. It is important to know who your allies are and how you can influence others to gain support for your project. The most productive ways to have influence are to have expertise related to the project and to use challenging work to motivate people.

OBJECTIVES ON THE JOB

Try to maintain executive support throughout the life of the project. If an executive is wavering on support, find out why and address the situation accordingly.

PRACTICE TEST QUESTIONS

1. **An executive who fully supported a project when it started is now wavering on that support. What would be the most likely reason for this change in behavior?**
   a. The executive may be going through a personal problem and not be able to make decisions rationally.
   b. The executive may realize that other issues have a higher priority to the organization now.
   c. The executive may be negotiating a job change and not want others to know about it.
   d. The executive may have a health problem and not want others to know about it.

2. **When do project managers and their teams most need executive support?**
   a. at project initiation
   b. during project planning
   c. during project execution
   d. throughout the life of the project

3. **What can a project manager do when an important executive is wavering on support of the project? Select three answers.**
   a. Identify the source of doubts.
   b. Use interpersonal communication skills to help win back support.
   c. Use allies and influence to help gain back support.
   d. Find a different executive to sponsor your project

4. **You are having major problems with a vendor. You have tried your best to resolve the problems, but you believe that a senior executive from your company should talk to a senior executive at the vendor's organization. Your main executive sponsor, however, does not seem interested in getting involved and rarely checks on the status of your project. What should you do?**
   a. Meet face-to-face with your executive sponsor to discuss the situation further.
   b. Meet yourself with the vendor's senior executive without getting your own senior management involved.
   c. Send a letter to the vendor's senior management threatening to cancel the contract.
   d. Send an e-mail to your executive sponsor's boss describing the sponsor's poor behavior.

5. **Which ways to have influence are usually the most effective? Select two answers.**
   a. using penalties
   b. having expertise
   c. having authority
   d. providing work challenge

3.6   Identify issues to consider when trying to get approval of a changed project plan that is still within expected budget, but has a schedule that extends outside of the original scope (e.g., the need to know and understand the proposed changes, the need to be able to justify and sell the changes, the need for alternative courses of action if the plan isn't accepted, etc.). Given a scenario involving a new project with an extended schedule, choose an appropriate course of action.

ADDRESSING ISSUES RELATED TO EXTENDING A PROJECT SCHEDULE

UNDERSTANDING THE OBJECTIVE

Project managers must manage scope, time, and cost goals for projects. Meeting schedule goals is often the most challenging of these goals. It is important to communicate the need to extend a project completion date to all affected stakeholders.

WHAT YOU REALLY NEED TO KNOW

- ◆ There are many reasons why a project schedule date might slip. If a project can still meet scope and cost goals, it should be easier to justify and handle a schedule increase. That is much more difficult when more than one project goal is not met.
- ◆ Issues to consider when trying to get approval for extending a project schedule include the following:
  - Impact on other project goals. If the schedule cannot be extended, can you still meet scope and/or cost goals?
  - Impact on the rest of the organization. If the schedule is delayed, will there be negative effects on other aspects of the organization? For example, will a late delivery cause the organization to be unable to compete for a new project or lose an important customer?
  - Impact on the project team. If the schedule is delayed, how does it affect the schedules of the people working on the project?
  - Impact on vendors. Do you need to change contracts or make special provision for vendors if the project schedule is delayed?
- ◆ If a project schedule must be delayed, the project manager must be able to explain the proposed changes and justify them to all affected stakeholders.
- ◆ If the project sponsor or other stakeholders refuse to accept a schedule delay, the project team should have some alternative courses of action, such as decreasing the scope of the project or increasing funding to meet the planned completion date.

OBJECTIVES ON THE JOB

If a project schedule must be delayed, have clear reasons for the delay. Also prepare alternative plans of action if the schedule cannot be delayed.

PRACTICE TEST QUESTIONS

1. **Which of the following are important issues to consider when trying to obtain approval to extend the project schedule? Select three answers.**
   - a. the impact on cost and scope
   - b. the impact on the rest of the organization
   - c. the impact on the project team
   - d. the impact on facilities

2. **You have been doing a great job managing a large information technology project. You are about halfway finished, and the cost and scope goals are right on target. You project, however, that the schedule will probably be delayed by a few months. What should you do? Select two answers.**
   - a. Continue the project as planned.
   - b. Prepare a justification for delaying the scheduled completion date.
   - c. Let all stakeholders know as soon as possible that the completion date has changed.
   - d. Prepare alternative courses of action if you cannot delay the completion date.

3. **You are managing a large information technology project. Everything has been going as planned, but recent information suggests that you can still meet scope and cost goals if you extend the completion date a few months. How can you justify slipping the schedule to your project sponsor?**
   - a. Explain that the scope goals can still be met with the delay.
   - b. Explain that the risk goals can still be met with the delay.
   - c. Explain that the time goals can still be met with the delay.
   - d. Explain that the procurement goals can still be met with the delay.

4. **You are managing a large information technology project. Everything has been going as planned, but recent information suggests that you can still meet scope and cost goals if you extend the completion date a few months. You have discussed the situation with your project sponsor, but he/she insists that you still meet the planned completion date. What should you do? Select two answers.**
   - a. Prepare alternative plans that will still allow the project to finish on time.
   - b. Reduce the quality of work so that the project can still finish on time.
   - c. Increase spending to finish on time.
   - d. Discuss options for completing the project with the sponsor.

5. **If you need to extend a project schedule, what normally happens?**
   - a. The cost and scope increase.
   - b. The cost and scope decrease.
   - c. Other parts of the organization are affected.
   - d. The project manager is reassigned.

OBJECTIVES

3.7   Define and explain the function of the following financial management variables: the cost performance index (CPI), schedule performance index (SPI), cost variance (CV), schedule variance (SV), percent spent, percent complete, and the to-complete performance index (TCPI). Explain how to track the financial performance of a project, given the financial management baseline for a project, using these variables.

TRACKING PROJECT PERFORMANCE USING EARNED VALUE MANAGEMENT

UNDERSTANDING THE OBJECTIVE
Earned value management is a project performance measurement technique that integrates scope, time, and cost data. After setting a baseline, you can enter actual performance information to see how the project is doing in meeting its goals (see ITPM2e, pp. 175-183).

WHAT YOU REALLY NEED TO KNOW

- A **baseline** is the original project plan plus approved changes. You must have a baseline to use earned value analysis.
- **Earned value** (**EV**), also called the budgeted cost of work performed (**BCWP**), is the percentage of work actually completed, multiplied by the planned value. **EV = PV * percent complete.**
- The **planned value** (**PV**), also called the budgeted cost of work scheduled (**BCWS**), is that portion of the approved total cost estimate planned to be spent on an activity during a given time period.
- The **actual cost** (**AC**), also called the actual cost of work performed (**ACWP**), is the total direct and indirect cost incurred in accomplished work on an activity during a given period of time.
- **Cost variance** (**CV**) is the earned value minus the actual cost. **CV = EV − AC. Schedule variance** (**SV**) is the earned value minus the planned value. **SV = EV − PV.**
- The **cost performance index** (**CPI**) is the ratio of earned value to actual cost. **CPI = EV/AC.** The **schedule performance index** (**SPI**) is the ratio of earned value to planned value. **SPI = EV/PV.**
- The **budget at completion** (**BAC**) is the original total budget for the project. The **Estimate at Completion** (**EAC**) can be calculated by dividing the BAC by the CPI. **EAC = BAC/CPI.**
- The **to-complete performance index** (**TCPI**) is used to determine what cost performance factor will be needed to complete all the remaining work according to a financial goal set by management. **TCPI = BAC − EV.**
- A negative cost or schedule variance means the project is over budget or behind schedule. A positive variance means the project is under budget or ahead of schedule. An index greater than or equal to 100% means the project's performance is equal to or better than planned, while an index less than 100% means performance is worse than planned.

OBJECTIVES ON THE JOB
Use earned value management to track project scope, time, and cost performance.

PRACTICE TEST QUESTIONS

1. **Which of the following items describe earned value? Select two answers.**
   a. the budgeted cost of work scheduled
   b. the budged cost of work performed
   c. the ratio of planned value to actual cost
   d. planned value times percent complete

2. **What performance measurement technique can you use to integrate scope, time, and cost data?**
   a. return on investment
   b. present value analysis
   c. economic value added
   d. earned value management

3. **If the BCWP is $10,000 and the ACWP is $8,000, what is the cost variance?**
   a. $2,000
   b. -$2,000
   c. 80%
   d. 125%

4. **If the EV is $20,000 and the SV is $25,000, what is the SPI?**
   a. $5,000
   b. -$5,000
   c. 80%
   d. 125%

5. **If the BAC is $200,000 and the CPI is 90%, what is the EAC?**
   a. $222,222
   b. $250,000
   c. $180,000
   d. $150,000

6. **If the BAC is $500,000 and the EV is $200,000, what is the TCPI?**
   a. $700,000
   b. 2.5
   c. 4.0
   d. $300,000

OBJECTIVES

3.8   Given an approved project plan and a specific scope deviation (for example: design change, schedule or cost change, etc.), demonstrate your ability to identify causes, prepare a status report for the user identifying problems and corrective action, determine the impact of the deviation on the scope of the project, quantify the deviation in terms of time, cost, and resources, distinguish between variances which will affect the budget and duration and those that will not. Also, determine and quantify at least one possible alternative solution that has less impact but requires some scope compromise, distinguish between variances that should be elevated to the sponsor and those that should be handled by the project manager and team, and develop a plan to gain stakeholder approval.

PERFORMING CHANGE CONTROL

UNDERSTANDING THE OBJECTIVE

Many information technology projects involve changes. It is important for project managers to be able to handle changes appropriately.

WHAT YOU REALLY NEED TO KNOW

◆ When changes occur on projects, project managers must do the following:
- Demonstrate their ability to identify causes.
- Prepare a status report for the user identifying problems and corrective action. A written status report is an important way to document scope changes.
- Determine the impact of the deviation on the scope of the project and quantify the deviation in terms of time, cost, and resources. Changes in scope normally cause changes in time, cost, and resources.
- Distinguish between variances that will affect the budget and duration and those that will not. Some changes will not affect the budget and schedule.
- Determine and quantify alternative solutions that have less impact but require scope compromise. Asking users to distinguish between mandatory and optional scope changes will help create alternative solutions.
- Distinguish between variances that should be elevated to the sponsor. Some decisions should be elevated to the project sponsor, especially if they cause significant changes to the scope, budget, or schedule for the project.
- Develop a plan to gain stakeholder approval. It is important to involve stakeholders in the change control process and plan for earning their approval.

OBJECTIVES ON THE JOB

Plan for and manage changes to project scope, time, and cost goals.

PRACTICE TEST QUESTIONS

1. **A senior developer on your project has found a major bug in a software module. You are supposed to freeze the code in a few days, but the developer says it will take at least a couple of weeks for proper fixing and testing of the bug. What should you do? Select two answers.**
   a. Ask the developer to fix the bug as well as possible, then freeze the code on time without the testing.
   b. Ask the developer to estimate whether taking the additional time now will affect the overall cost or schedule for the project.
   c. Talk to affected stakeholders and suggest a few weeks' extension to fix and test the bug before freezing the code.
   d. Issue a change order, since the work is out of project scope.

2. **How should you communicate important changes to the scope of a project? Select two answers.**
   a. Put important changes in writing.
   b. Verbally tell affected stakeholders of the changes in a timely manner.
   c. Document the changes in a daily change log.
   d. Document all changes in a contract.

3. **What do major changes in information technology project scopes normally affect? Select three answers.**
   a. budget
   b. quality
   c. schedule
   d. resources

4. **An important project stakeholder has submitted a major scope change request for your project. Your team estimates that incorporating all of the proposed changes would cause major time and cost increases. What could you do to develop alternative solutions that have less impact?**
   a. Ask the stakeholder to distinguish between mandatory and optional scope changes in the proposal.
   b. Ask the stakeholder to provide detailed time and cost estimates along with the proposed scope changes.
   c. Ask the stakeholder to submit half the original proposed changes.

5. **When should you involve stakeholders in the change control process on projects?**
   a. before a change is submitted
   b. after a change is submitted
   c. when a change is submitted
   d. throughout the life of the project

6. **When should you elevate a proposed scope change to the project sponsor? Select two answers.**
   a. whenever a change is submitted
   b. whenever a change is approved
   c. when a change significantly impacts project cost
   d. when a change significantly impacts the schedule

OBJECTIVES

3.9　Identify and justify the following as conditions for initiating a change control process: resource changes, schedule changes, cost changes, requirements changes or changes in expectations, infrastructure changes, and as a response to scope creep.

IDENTIFYING AND JUSTIFYING CONDITIONS FOR INITIATING A CHANGE CONTROL PROCESS

UNDERSTANDING THE OBJECTIVE

Information technology projects often involve changes. The change control process involves identifying, evaluating, and managing changes throughout the project life cycle. It is important for project managers to understand this process and determine if changes have occurred or should occur (see ITPM2e, p. 71-76).

WHAT YOU REALLY NEED TO KNOW

◆ The main objectives of the change control process are:

- Influencing the factors that create changes to ensure that changes are beneficial. Project managers and their teams must make trade-offs among key project dimensions such as scope, time cost, and quality. If a proposed change can positively affect any of these dimensions, the changes should be encouraged. For example, there may be a cheaper hardware solution than what was planned. If proposed changes have a negative affect on any of these dimensions, those affects must be explained.

- Determining that a change has occurred. The project manager must know the status of key project areas at all times and communicate changes to major stakeholders. Project team members may quit; direct costs may increase; the organization may undergo infrastructure changes; or a vendor supplying equipment for the project may go out of business. It is important for the project manager to keep his/her eye on the big picture of the project and know when changes occur.

- Managing actual changes as they occur. It is important that project managers exercise discipline in managing the project to help minimize the number of changes that occur. When changes are needed, the project manager must justify and manage the changes.

◆ The change control process may be initiated as a response to changes in resources, schedules, costs, requirements, expectations, infrastructure, or as a response to scope creep. It is important for project managers and their teams to be aware of all types of changes.

◆ Many information technology projects suffer from **scope creep**, the tendency for scope to keep getting bigger and bigger (see ITPM2e, p. 107). If scope creep occurs, the project manager must mange the growth in scope through the change control process.

OBJECTIVES ON THE JOB

Know when and how to initiate the change control process.

PRACTICE TEST QUESTIONS

1. **Which of the following areas might cause the change control process to be initiated? Select three answers.**
   a. resource changes
   b. performance tracking changes
   c. project manager changes
   d. infrastructure changes
   e. changes in expectations

2. **Which of the following conditions for initiating a change control process generally results in increased costs and/or schedules?**
   a. resource changes
   b. scope creep
   c. quality control
   d. changes in expectations

3. **What type of changes should project managers encourage?**
   a. changes that result from resource variations
   b. changes that result from scope creep
   c. changes that positively impact scope, time, or cost goals
   d. changes that follow the standard change control process

4. **How can project managers stay abreast of changes affecting their projects? Select two answers.**
   a. Require that all proposed changes go through a formal change control process.
   b. Stay aware of project status by requiring status information for all key project areas.
   c. Keep their eyes on the big project picture.
   d. Sit on the change control board.

5. **You have been asked to lead a project that was initiated over a year ago. The project scope, time, and cost estimates have been revised many times, and the team seems confused. Users bring new requests to the developers on a daily basis. What should you do? Select two answers.**
   a. Do not accept any more changes to the project.
   b. Require that all changes go through a change control board.
   c. Hold a project review meeting to clarify the current goals of the project.
   d. Have key stakeholders sign off on the current project goals.

6. **Which characteristic of a project manager helps to minimize scope creep?**
   a. communications skills
   b. discipline
   c. honesty
   d. intelligence

OBJECTIVES

3.10 Given scenarios involving requests for changes from sponsors, team members or third parties, recognize and explain how to prevent scope creep.

RECOGNIZING AND PREVENTING SCOPE CREEP

UNDERSTANDING THE OBJECTIVE

The first step in preventing scope creep is recognizing it. It is important to verify the project scope and develop a process for controlling scope changes. On information technology projects, it is crucial to have good user input and to reduce incomplete and changing requirements in order to help prevent scope creep.

WHAT YOU REALLY NEED TO KNOW

◆ Scope verification involves formal acceptance of the project scope by the stakeholders. An important step in identifying and preventing scope creep is having stakeholders verify the project scope. The project scope should be well documented in the planning phases of the project.

◆ The project team should have clear descriptions of the project's products and procedures for determining whether they were completed correctly and satisfactorily.

◆ To verify scope and control scope change, it is important to have good user input and to reduce incomplete and changing requirements.

◆ Suggestions for improving user input include developing a good project selection process, having users on the project team, holding regular meetings, delivering something to users and sponsors on a regular basis, and co-locating users with developers (see ITPM2e, p. 109).

◆ Suggestions for reducing incomplete and changing requirements include developing and following a requirements management process, using techniques such as prototyping, use case modeling, and Joint Application Design (JAD) to help understand user requirements, putting all requirements in writing and keeping them current, creating a requirements management database, providing adequate testing to verify that projects perform as expected, using a process for reviewing requested requirements changes from a systems perspective, and emphasizing completion dates (see ITPM2e, p. 109-111).

OBJECTIVES ON THE JOB

Use several strategies to help prevent scope creep, such as verifying project scope, improving user input, and reducing incomplete and changing requirements.

PRACTICE TEST QUESTIONS

1. **You are just about to begin executing a large software development project. You have a detailed scope statement and WBS, but there was never any verification of the scope with key stakeholders. What should you do?**
   a. Skip the scope verification and continue with the project execution.
   b. Perform scope verification first to ensure key stakeholders accept the project scope.
   c. Issue a fee for any changes to the existing project scope.
   d. Sign a scope verification form yourself and put it on file.

2. **Which of the following is important for verifying scope and controlling scope changes on an information technology project?**
   a. having the most productive users on the project
   b. improving user input on the project
   c. reducing project requirements
   d. reducing incomplete and changing requirements

3. **How can you improve user input on a project? Select two answers.**
   a. Require user signatures on all scope-related documents.
   b. Have users on the project team.
   c. Co-locate users and developers.
   d. Screen users more carefully.

4. **Which of the following techniques can be used to help manage requirements? Select three answers.**
   a. prototyping
   b. use case modeling
   c. JAD
   d. worst case modeling

5. **You have managed many large information technology projects, and you have found that it is much better to emphasize completion dates than to focus on meeting all project requirements. Which of the following best describes your management philosophy?**
   a. Sacrifice some functionality for schedule.
   b. Sacrifice pleasing stakeholders for schedule.
   c. Please stakeholders by staying on budget.
   d. The project manager has legitimate power.

6. **You seem to be spending most of your time dealing with potential scope changes on your project. What can you do to reduce incomplete and changing requirements? Select three answers.**
   a. Put all requirements in writing and keep them current.
   b. Create a requirements management database.
   c. Create an entity relationship diagram.
   d. Emphasize completion dates.
   e. Use a shorter testing process.

3.11 Recognize and explain the importance of communicating significant proposed changes in project scope, and their impacts, to management, and getting management review and approval.

COMMUNICATING PROPOSED SCOPE CHANGES TO MANAGEMENT AND GETTING MANAGEMENT APPROVAL

UNDERSTANDING THE OBJECTIVE

Senior managers hate surprises. Project managers must communicate significant proposed changes to the project sponsor and other affected senior managers. It is important to emphasize the reason for changes and any impacts they may have on other areas.

WHAT YOU REALLY NEED TO KNOW

- ◆ Several project stakeholders are in senior management positions:
  - Functional managers. Most information technology project teams involve people from several departments. The functional managers in charge of those departments (marketing, sales, engineering, human resources, etc.) must be informed of major changes to a project. They might want to reallocate their resources on the basis of those changes.
  - Senior managers. The project sponsor is often a senior manager, either within the company or from a customer organization. Senior managers in particular need to make sure that all projects are coordinated and continue to serve the best interests of the entire organization.
  - Vendor managers. Many information technology projects involve purchasing goods and services from vendors. The managers at those companies want to know if any project changes affect their delivery schedules, costs, or workloads.
- ◆ When communicating significant proposed changes to senior managers, it is important to emphasize the reason for the change and the impact of the change.
- ◆ Project managers must get management review and approval of major project changes. Changes often require more money and/or time, and senior management can authorize the use of more funds and/or extend project deadlines.
- ◆ Project managers should keep senior management informed of project progress periodically throughout the life of the project so proposed changes are not total surprises. Senior management should be involved in defining changes and have final approval of them.

OBJECTIVES ON THE JOB

Always keep senior managers informed of project progress, and do not surprise them with sudden changes. Justify changes and explain the rationale behind them and how they will impact the rest of the project and the organization.

PRACTICE TEST QUESTIONS

1. **Which of the following stakeholders on a large information technology project are normally considered to be senior managers? Select three answers.**
   a. the project manager assigned to the project
   b. functional managers who have personnel assigned to the project
   c. the project sponsor
   d. vendor managers
   e. users

2. **The business environment has caused major changes in the scope of your project. Why should you inform functional managers about these scope changes? Select two answers.**
   a. All affected senior managers should be informed of project progress periodically.
   b. The functional managers are paying for part of the project, so they should be informed of scope changes.
   c. The functional managers should be involved in writing the new specifications.
   d. The functional managers may want to reallocate their people who are assigned to the project.

3. **Your company is going through a major restructuring that will significantly affect the scope of the current project you are managing. When should you inform vendor managers supporting your project about this scope change?**
   a. You do not need to Inform vendor managers.
   b. When the vendor delivers its next major product.
   c. When you pay the vendor its next progress payment.
   d. As soon as possible.

4. **Your project requires a significant change in scope to meet changing business and technology needs. You are not sure yet how much change is involved, and your project sponsor has asked your team to work with the users to develop some alternatives. Your company believes in a decentralized decision-making process. As project manager, whom would you have working on the scope changes? Put the following stakeholders in order, based on the timing of their involvement in developing the scope changes.**
   a. sponsor
   b. vendor managers
   c. senior managers
   d. project team and users

5. **What should you emphasize when communicating a significant proposed change in scope to senior managers? Select two answers.**
   a. the effect of the change on project staffing
   b. the rationale for the changes
   c. the technical reasons for the changes
   d. the impact of the changes on the rest of the project and the organization

OBJECTIVES

3.12 Identify and explain strategies for maintaining qualified deliverables, given a large project with many team members at multiple locations (e.g., communication standards, work standards, etc.).

IDENTIFYING AND EXPLAINING STRATEGIES FOR MAINTAINING QUALIFIED DELIVERABLES ON LARGE PROJECTS

UNDERSTANDING THE OBJECTIVE

The larger the project, the more difficult it is to manage. The same is true for the number of locations involved in the project. It is important for project managers to develop a strategy for ensuring that quality deliverables are provided on time and in budget to keep large and/or multiple-location projects running smoothly.

WHAT YOU REALLY NEED TO KNOW

- ◆ Large projects present unique challenges to project managers. With more people and tasks involved, communications becomes even more important.
- ◆ Projects involving multiple locations also present challenges to project managers.
- ◆ There are several strategies for handling large and/or multiple location projects:
  - Develop standards for communications. To avoid confusion and streamline communications, many large projects require all stakeholders to use specific standards for communicating information. For example, everyone may be required to enter project information into and track it on the same project management software system. The project may have templates for key project documents that everyone must follow. There may be a communication media grid suggesting when to use various media—written reports, face-to-face meetings, e-mail, web sites, videoconferencing, etc.—to communicate information.
  - Develop work standards. Another strategy involves creating and following specific standards of work performance. For example, specific testing procedures might be required for all software development on a project.
  - Create subteams. Break down the management of the project into subteams. Each sub-team is responsible for specific tasks and deliverables, and the subteam manager coordinates information through the project manager.
  - Focus on milestones. To keep large and/or multiple-location projects on track, it often helps to focus on achieving milestones, such as providing deliverables.
- ◆ To ensure quality deliverables are provided on time and within budget, project managers must emphasize that deliverables are well defined and tracked. There should be interim milestones to ensure deliverables will meet expectations.

OBJECTIVES ON THE JOB

Identify and implement appropriate strategies when working on large and/or multiple-location projects.

PRACTICE TEST QUESTIONS

1. **What types of projects are generally more difficult to manage? Select two answers.**
   a. large projects
   b. small projects
   c. single-location projects
   d. multiple-location projects

2. **What strategies can you use to help manage large and/or multiple-location projects? Select three answers.**
   a. require all work be posted on a common web site
   b. develop standards for communications
   c. develop standards for work
   d. create subteams

3. **You are the project manager for a large project with users and team members at multiple geographic locations. What type of reports should you focus on to keep the big picture in mind?**
   a. status reports
   b. progress reports
   c. deliverable reports
   d. milestone reports

4. **What should you do to ensure that your large project maintains qualified deliverables? Select three answers.**
   a. Hire a deliverable review consultant.
   b. Emphasize that deliverables are well defined.
   c. Track the progress of all deliverables.
   d. Have interim milestones to ensure deliverables will meet expectations.

5. **You are managing a large software development project. You have teams of developers working at multiple locations. You are requiring all teams to use specific testing procedures. What strategy are you using to ensure quality deliverables?**
   a. corporate standards
   b. work standards
   c. communications standards
   d. quality control

6. **What can you do to provide standards for project communications on a large, multiple-location project? Select two answers.**
   a. Use a common project management software system.
   b. Provide templates for key project documents.
   c. Require monthly face-to-face meetings.
   d. Require monthly teleconferencing meetings.

3.13 Recognize and explain the importance of quality testing in situations where tasks are being performed both by project team members and by third parties.

USING QUALITY TESTING WITH TEAM MEMBERS AND THIRD PARTIES

UNDERSTANDING THE OBJECTIVE

Many software related projects involve development and testing of software by both the project team and third parties, such as vendors or consultants. It is important to define and follow quality testing procedures to make sure the software works properly.

WHAT YOU REALLY NEED TO KNOW

◆ Many information technology projects involve testing software.
- **Unit testing** is done to test each individual component (often a program) to ensure it is as defect-free as possible.
- **Integration testing** occurs between unit and system testing to test functionally grouped components. It ensures subset(s) of the entire system work together.
- **System testing** tests the entire system as one entity.
- **User acceptance testing** is an independent test performed by end users prior to accepting the delivered system.
- **Verification or alpha testing runs the system in a simulated environment using simulated data.**
- **Validation or beta testing** runs the system in a live environment using real data.
- **Audit testing** certifies that the system is free of errors and is ready to be put into operation.

◆ When both project team members and third parties perform software development and/or testing, it is even more important to follow a detailed, disciplined testing process to ensure software quality. **Third parties** can be vendors, consulting firms, individual consultants, or independent testing agencies.

◆ Quality managers ensure that proper procedures are followed. Many organizations use software to assist in developing and testing software. Developers often have to check in new code after is has been tested locally, and test scripts are followed to make sure the code does not cause problems in other parts of the system.

◆ For large software development projects, it is often helpful to have an outside organization assist in the testing process. Be sure the outside organization is well respected and familiar with the type of project you are managing.

OBJECTIVES ON THE JOB

Don't short-change testing. Plan and follow a disciplined testing process, especially when projects involve both third parties and the project team in development.

PRACTICE TEST QUESTIONS

1. **Match each type of testing to its description.**

Audit testing	a.	Alpha testing
Validation testing	b.	Beta testing
Unit testing	c.	Ensures each program is as defect-free as possible
Verification testing	d.	Certifies the system is ready to be put into operation.

2. **What third parties might be involved in testing? Select three answers.**
   - a. the project team
   - b. vendors
   - c. consulting firms
   - d. independent testing agencies

3. **Who is directly responsible for ensuring that proper testing procedures are followed on a software development project?**
   - a. the lead software developer
   - b. the quality manager
   - c. the auditor
   - d. third parties

4. **You are overseeing a large project that involves a significant amount of software development. You have several vendors and members of your project team working on the development. You know that proper testing is essential. What could you consider to help the testing process?**
   - a. Have senior management sign off on the test plans.
   - b. Hire a respected outside organization to assist in the testing process.
   - c. Require regression testing.
   - d. Require the vendors to collocate with your developers.

5. **What type of testing is done to certify that the system is free of errors and is ready to be placed into operation?**
   - a. system testing
   - b. user acceptance testing
   - c. validation testing
   - d. audit testing

6. **What type of testing runs the system in a live environment using real data?**
   - a. system testing
   - b. user acceptance testing
   - c. validation testing
   - d. audit testing

OBJECTIVES

3.14 Identify and explain strategies for assuring quality during the turnover phase (e.g., user documentation, user training, helpdesk training, support structure, etc.).

IDENTIFYING AND EXPLAINING STRATEGIES FOR ASSURING QUALITY DURING THE TURNOVER PHASE

UNDERSTANDING THE OBJECTIVE

After information technology projects are complete, they usually become part of normal operations in an organization. It is crucial to plan for the turnover of the new products and services produced by the project.

WHAT YOU REALLY NEED TO KNOW

◆ Many information technology projects result in the creation of new products or services. Since projects are finite by definition, it is important to plan for the transition of the required support of these products and services within the organization. This transition work is often part of the main project, or it can be another project in itself.

◆ Some of the transition work involved in information technology projects includes the following:

- User documentation. New hardware, software, and networks need good user documentation, even though many information technology professionals may dislike writing it. Technical writers often provide assistance in creating and/or editing user documentation, as do users themselves.

- User training. It is crucial to provide good training for users. Training takes many forms, including instructor-led training, computer-based training, and one-on-one training. The project team should clarify training needs early in the project and ensure that training is effective in helping users learn new systems.

- Helpdesk training. No matter how user-friendly systems are, there is still a need for helpdesk support. Helpdesk staff must understand the new systems very well, enjoy working with people, and be able to trouble-shoot user problems. It is important to train helpdesk employees so they can quickly and effectively help users.

◆ It is also important to plan and implement a support structure for the new systems created. There may be a need to create a new organizational unit and/or hire new staff to support the new systems.

OBJECTIVES ON THE JOB

Be sure to plan for a smooth transition of new information systems into the organization. Users need documentation, training, and helpdesk support.

PRACTICE TEST QUESTIONS

1. **Which of the following normally is done in the turnover phase of an information technology project? Select two answers.**
   a. user documentation
   b. testing
   c. training
   d. quality control

2. **In which project phase do you create user documentation and provide user and helpdesk training?**
   a. planning
   b. passover
   c. turnover
   d. support

3. **Your project team is nearing the end of a large system development project. The manager in charge of the department using the new system asks you when the user training sessions will be held. You tell him/her that training was not part of your project plan. The manager is confused and upset. What should you do?**
   a. Add training to your existing project.
   b. Ask for senior management approval to add training to your existing project.
   c. Tell the manager to ask the existing IT department staff to provide the training.
   d. Tell the manager that the system is so friendly that no training is needed.

4. **Your project team is developing training for the helpdesk staff that will be supporting the new system your project produced. Which of the following skills should you include in the training? Select three answers.**
   a. technical training on how to use the new system
   b. documentation training on how to document the new system
   c. communication training to help staff work with users
   d. trouble-shooting training to identify and solve technical problems

5. **What additional work may be required at the end of a project when new products and services are produced? Select two answers.**
   a. The organization may need to create a new unit or department to support the new products and services.
   b. The organization may need to hire outside consultants to assess the value of the new products and services.
   c. The organization may need to hire new staff to support the new products and services.

OBJECTIVES

3.15 Identify strategies for providing constructive, timely performance feedback to a multi-geographical project team with diverse skills, doing it in such a way that it enhances each individual team member's value to the project.

IDENTIFYING STRATEGIES FOR PROVIDING PERFORMANCE FEEDBACK TO DIVERSE PROJECT TEAMS

UNDERSTANDING THE OBJECTIVE

People make or break projects, and it is important to treat them well. People need feedback to know that their work is valued and that they are doing it up to expectations. It is important to understand each individual on a project team, even when they are geographically dispersed, and to provide timely performance feedback.

WHAT YOU REALLY NEED TO KNOW

◆ Projects are broken down into specific tasks that are done by specific people. It is crucial for project managers to provide constructive, timely performance feedback to every employee.

◆ On very large projects, there are often subteam managers or team leads reporting to the project manager. These managers often provide feedback to their team members, but the project manager should be as involved as possible in motivating every team member.

◆ It is important to understand individuals' needs when providing feedback. People have different skills, personalities, and motivational needs. Feedback should be constructive and focus on improving performance.

◆ For project team members in different geographical locations, project managers often have to rely on written and verbal communications, rather than face-to-face communications. It is important to have clear goals for each team member in order to provide feedback on achieving those goals.

◆ Team members often have very diverse skill levels. Less skilled employees may require more feedback than more experienced ones. Project managers should strive to help people develop their skills and be sensitive to individual needs.

◆ Some organizations have set time periods for performance feedback, but most companies have a minimum of one review a year. Project managers should provide both annual performance feedback and ongoing feedback for effective management of the project.

OBJECTIVES ON THE JOB

Everyone needs feedback. Focus on providing feedback that will enhance individual and team performance.

PRACTICE TEST QUESTIONS

1. **When giving feedback to project team members, what should you strive for? Select two answers.**
   a. pointing out weaknesses that should be addressed
   b. providing constructive suggestions
   c. enhancing each individual team member's value to the project
   d. not offending anyone because of his or her cultural values

2. **You are managing a large project with over fifty full-time project personnel. You underestimated how much time it would take you to provide formal and informal performance feedback, but you know how important it is. What should you do?**
   a. Ask your team leads to provide performance feedback to their people.
   b. Use an automated system for providing the performance feedback.
   c. Provide group versus individual feedback.
   d. Provide feedback only once a year instead of twice a year.

3. **Several key members of your project team work almost exclusively in a virtual environment. You are used to providing feedback face-to-face, but you have never even met some of these people. How can you provide meaningful feedback? Select two answers.**
   a. Have clear goals for each team member.
   b. Use videoconferencing when providing feedback to geographically dispersed team members.
   c. Insist on having face-to-face meetings periodically with all team members.
   d. Have feedback focus on performance rather than meeting individual goals.

4. **Your software developers have a wide range of skills. How should you handle providing performance feedback for them?**
   a. Provide feedback more often for highly skilled developers.
   b. Provide feedback more often for less skilled developers.
   c. Provide the same amount of feedback to all developers.

5. **How often should you provide performance feedback to project team members?**
   a. weekly
   b. monthly
   c. whenever it is needed, but at least once a year
   d. whenever there is a performance problem

OBJECTIVES

3.16 Given disgruntled employees who are affecting team morale, demonstrate an understanding of when to encourage, punish, or reassign people and how to address these issues/situations within the team to restore team morale.

HANDLING DISGRUNTLED EMPLOYEES

UNDERSTANDING THE OBJECTIVE

It is always difficult to deal with disgruntled employees. Project managers must focus on meeting project objectives, and disgruntled employees often hurt team morale. There are several strategies for handling these difficult situations.

WHAT YOU REALLY NEED TO KNOW

- ◆ Employees may be disgruntled or unhappy for many different reasons. It is usually fairly easy to identify a disgruntled employee, but finding the cause for his/her unhappiness can be very difficult.

- ◆ Project managers should address the problem with other members of the team and strive to keep team morale high. The negative attitudes of one person should not pull down the whole team.

- ◆ Project managers and/or team leads should talk to disgruntled employees in an effort to understand the reasons for their unhappiness. Sometimes people just need more encouragement to work harder and be more supportive of a project.

- ◆ In some cases you cannot change the behavior of a disgruntled employee. If positive reinforcement or motivational efforts do not work, the project manager may need to punish or reassign the employee. Punishments can take many forms, such as pay cuts, undesirable assignments, or relocation. Sometimes the employee must be reassigned away from the project team or even fired from the organization.

- ◆ Project managers must work with functional managers and human resource managers to understand the organizational policies related to problem employees. There may be special social services, training, or counseling available to help the employee. Project managers also need to understand processes for reassigning or firing employees that will not result in potential litigation.

OBJECTIVES ON THE JOB

It is difficult to work with disgruntled employees. Project managers must take actions to avoid hurting team morale and performance.

PRACTICE TEST QUESTIONS

1. **What is the term used to describe an employee with a very negative attitude toward his/her job?**
   a. pessimistic
   b. disgruntled
   c. depressed
   d. ungrateful

2. **Why are some employees disgruntled?**
   a. They are underpaid.
   b. They are overworked.
   c. They do not like their coworkers.
   d. There are many reasons.

3. **One person on your project team has a very negative attitude toward your project and the company. This person has been with the company for over five years, and he/she does have some valuable skills. However, the morale of the project team is suffering. Put the following steps in order to indicate how you would handle this situation.**
   a. reassign or fire the employee.
   b. provide incentives to help change the employee's behavior.
   c. talk one-on-one with the disgruntled employee about the problem.
   d. work with your human resources department to provide special training or counseling services for the employee.

4. **You have met with a disgruntled employee on your project team. Even though his/her work is acceptable and you have provided incentives to change his/her negative attitude, other team members are still complaining about this person. You are considering some form of punishment when this employee exhibits negative behavior. Which of the following might be appropriate punishments? Select three answers.**
   a. verbal reprimands
   b. financial penalties
   c. taking away the person's computer
   d. relocating the employee's desk

5. **Why should you discuss a disgruntled employee with someone in the human resources department? Select three answers.**
   a. The human resources department should handle the situation.
   b. The human resources department may have some courses the employee could attend.
   c. The human resources department may provide special counseling services that could help the situation.
   d. The human resource department can explain acceptable procedures to follow and help avoid potential litigation.

OBJECTIVES

3.17 Given a management scenario in which there are individual performance problems, demonstrate how to recognize and understand issues, conditions, and underlying problems, and identify corrective actions that will help the employee return to productivity, including situations such as that of a top performer who has started to slack off or an individual who reports to the manager substandard performance on the part of another person.

HANDLING INDIVIDUAL PERFORMANCE PROBLEMS

UNDERSTANDING THE OBJECTIVE

An important part of being a project manager is motivating employees and dealing with performance problems. Project managers must recognize and understand the issues, conditions, and underlying problems related to performance problems, and take corrective actions.

WHAT YOU REALLY NEED TO KNOW

◆ Every project manager dreams of a team that never has performance problems, but an important part of any management position is dealing with performance problems.

◆ Project managers must be able to do the following:

- Recognize and understand the issues, conditions, and underlying problems causing the performance problems. The project manager must be aware of unique factors that can affect performance on each particular project. Is the team being forced to use outdated technology? Is there enough money for necessary training for team members? Is the company's pay structure affecting performance? Is a particular individual having family or health problems?

- Take corrective actions. The project manager should work with the team or affected individual to help improve performance. There are often several options to help improve performance, such as clarifying performance goals, providing necessary training or support, and providing motivation.

◆ A couple of common performance problems include:

- A top performer who has started to slack off. Most top performers are highly skilled and motivated individuals. When they slack off, there is usually a good reason for it. Perhaps the person needs a vacation or time off. Perhaps the person is becoming bored and needs more challenging work.

- Substandard performance of some team members. It is difficult to handle low performers, especially if another individual reports the substandard performance. This situation normally shows that the low performer is affecting other team members. The project manager should meet individually with low performers to try to help them, but in some cases they must be reassigned.

OBJECTIVES ON THE JOB

Recognize and manage performance problems, keeping the best interests of the project in mind.

PRACTICE TEST QUESTIONS

1. **You have just accepted the role of project manager on a large information technology project in the execution phase. You are reviewing some of your team's work, and you are surprised at the poor quality of the status reports and other written documentation. Before you confront your team, what should you do?**
   a. Explore the conditions of the project before you joined the team.
   b. Talk to the project sponsor to see if he/she agrees that the quality is poor.
   c. Fire the technical writers.
   d. Discretely provide samples of well written documentation.

2. **You have just accepted the role of project manager on a large information technology project in the execution phase. You are reviewing some of your team's work, and you are surprised at the poor quality of the written reports, especially the user documentation. What should you do? Select two answers.**
   a. Meet with key team members to discuss the problem.
   b. Reassign all writing to the technical writers supporting the project.
   c. See if there is a writing workshop that key team members could attend.
   d. Outsource important deliverables that involve a lot of writing.

3. **A few of your project team members are having performance problems. What are some options you can take to improve their performance? Select three answers.**
   a. Clarify performance goals.
   b. Provide necessary training or support.
   c. Set policies punishing poor performance.
   d. Provide incentives to improve performance.

4. **One of your top software developers is suddenly slacking off. Your project is about to enter an extremely critical phase, and you are depending on this person to perform. What should you do?**
   a. Remind the developer that he/she has work to do.
   b. Meet with the developer to find the source of the problem.
   c. Suggest the developer take a week's vacation to re-energize.
   d. Assign the developer to another part of the project.

5. **A member of your project team has reported another team member's substandard performance to his/her functional boss. What should you do?**
   a. Let the functional manager handle the problem.
   b. Reassign both of the team members.
   c. Reassign the team member with substandard performance.
   d. Meet with the supposed substandard performer to discuss the problem.

3.18 Given need to make up severe schedule slippage, demonstrate understanding of how to lead the project team through an extended overtime period, including how to motivate and reward, how to show sensitivity to individuals, and how to lead rather than push.

LEADING A PROJECT TEAM THROUGH AN EXTENDED OVERTIME PERIOD

UNDERSTANDING THE OBJECTIVE

Sometimes overtime cannot be avoided. Project managers may be required to lead their teams through an extended period of overtime to meet important project deadlines. It is important to provide strong motivation while being sensitive to individual needs in such situations.

WHAT YOU REALLY NEED TO KNOW

◆ Even if a project is well planned and executed, there are some situations where the team must work overtime for a period of time to provide quality products on time. Project managers should work with their teams to determine when overtime is needed and to plan ahead as much as possible. The team should state specific goals for the extended overtime period and track progress toward meeting those goals.

◆ It is important to be consistent and fair in determining overtime procedures, if possible. The particular project and organizational context often determine the best way to handle overtime. For example, it may work well to require all full-time project team members to work the same amount of overtime hours. If some employees are not paid overtime and others are, however, this policy may not work. If some employees are not needed during the overtime period, it does not make sense to have them work extra hours.

◆ It is also crucial to understand and manage individual needs during extended periods of overtime. Employees with young children, aging parents, medical problems, or other personal situations may not be able to work as much overtime as others. Employees working on degrees, practicing certain religious beliefs, or involved in important activities outside of work may also require special consideration.

◆ Project managers should discuss alternatives for getting the required work done. Perhaps some people could put in extra hours at home rather than spending more hours in the office. Some people might prefer to work the extra hours on a Saturday versus during the week. Providing flexibility often helps meet individual and work needs.

◆ Providing challenging work and recognition are strong motivators. Project managers should stress the importance of the work and challenge people to get it done. They should also lead by example and put forth their own best efforts during the crucial overtime period. When the job is completed, project personnel should be publicly recognized for their hard work.

◆ Financial incentives can also motivate people to work, especially to work overtime. If you cannot pay for overtime, consider providing comp time, meaning people can take those overtime hours off in the future.

OBJECTIVES ON THE JOB

Strong leadership is especially important during periods of extended overtime. Manage overtime well, be sensitive to individual needs, and lead by example.

PRACTICE TEST QUESTIONS

1. **You have asked your entire project team to work overtime for the next month to get an important project deliverable done on time. What can you do to make sure the overtime period is productive? Select two answers.**
   a. State specific goals for what needs to be accomplished.
   b. Provide free food for everyone during the overtime period.
   c. Provide free massages for everyone during the overtime period.
   d. Track progress toward meeting goals during the overtime period.

2. **You are managing a large project, and you and many of your team members must work overtime for the next month to meet an important deadline. Some of your team members are salaried and do not get any overtime pay, while others receive time-and-a-half for overtime. What can you do to entice the salaried workers to put in enough overtime?**
   a. Remind them that they are already well paid.
   b. Remind them that working extra hours is expected of salaried employees.
   c. Offer them a big bonus, even though you don't have authority to do so.
   d. Offer them comp time that they can use in the future.

3. **Your project team has agreed that everyone will work an equal amount of overtime when it is needed. Your company recently hired the CEO's nephew, and he has been assigned to your team. He was told by one interviewer that he would never have to work overtime unless he wanted to. What should you do?**
   a. Don't worry about it until an overtime period is required.
   b. Confront the CEO about this unfair treatment.
   c. Let all project team members know about team policies, including overtime.
   d. Have the head of human resources write a special employee contract for your team members.

4. **Your project team has been working overtime for a few weeks now. One of your lead developers comes to talk to you about the stress the overtime is putting on her and her family. What should you do? Select two answers.**
   a. Tell her that everyone must put in an equal amount of overtime to be fair.
   b. Suggest she take some stress management courses offered free by the company.
   c. Develop some alternatives for her particular situation.
   d. Suggest that she try to do some extra work at home whenever it is convenient.

5. **A couple of your team members have religious beliefs that prevent them from working on certain days. It is important to have them and everyone else work full-time plus overtime this next week. What should you do?**
   a. Tell everyone they must work or be fired.
   b. Honor individual religious beliefs and let them have time off as needed.
   c. Honor religious beliefs, but ask that everyone put in the necessary hours using flex time.
   d. Let everyone have those religious holidays off.

3.19 Given team performance problems and the causes, demonstrate the ability to develop a plan to address/correct the cause of the problem, including situations where the team is not focused and is pulling in different directions or where the team is fragmented into special interests or social groups and not united.

DEMONSTRATING THE ABILITY TO LEAD A TEAM THAT IS
UNFOCUSED OR FRAGMENTED

UNDERSTANDING THE OBJECTIVE

There are many reasons why teams may be having performance problems. Two particular problems projects managers need to address are an unfocused team and a fragmented team.

WHAT YOU REALLY NEED TO KNOW

◆ When a project team has performance problems, project managers must develop a plan to address the cause of the problem. Communications skills are crucial. The project manager should talk to affected individuals and the whole team as needed.

◆ Two common causes of performance problems include:

- The team is not focused or is pulling in different directions. It is crucial for all project team members to work toward common goals. If the team is not focused on common goals, project success is unlikely. The project manager must pull the team together and emphasize the goals of the project. If people disagree on the goals or how to achieve them, the project manager should call a special meeting with the sponsor and key stakeholders to clarify project goals.

- The team is fragmented into special interests or social groups. Unfortunately, project team members sometimes act like junior-high students instead of working adults. They may form cliques and focus on keeping their political or social groups intact instead of doing what is best for the project. In this situation, the project manager should again emphasize that everyone must focus on meeting project goals versus individual or subgroup goals. In severe cases, the project manager may need to reassign individuals to break up unproductive teams.

◆ Project managers must be aware of political and social aspects of their own project teams. Spending time in team-building activities early in a project can help to form team cohesiveness. More team-building activities can also be used if team-related problems surface.

◆ Project managers should remember that they can get assistance, if needed, from other people in the organization. The human resources department can provide facilitators to help dysfunctional teams, and functional or senior managers can also help resolve problems with specific individuals.

OBJECTIVES ON THE JOB

Projects run much more smoothly when the project team is focused and united in meeting project goals. If there are problems, project managers must address them and seek assistance, if needed.

PRACTICE TEST QUESTIONS

1. **Which of the following might be signs that your project team is unfocused on meeting project goals? Select two answers.**
   a. People are taking long lunches and working short days.
   b. People are not showing up for important meetings.
   c. People are working extra hours.
   d. People are using the Internet for personal reasons during lunch hour.

2. **You realize that members of your project team are not focused and are pulling in different directions. What should you do? Select two answers.**
   a. Schedule an off-site team-building activity as soon as possible.
   b. Call a special meeting of key project stakeholders to clarify project goals.
   c. Emphasize project goals and specific work assignments.
   d. Start a new policy of punishing people who do not act as team players.

3. **You have taken over the role of project manager for an important project. At the first team meeting, it is obvious that there are separate factions within the team. You later find out that there are some subgroups based on social and political interests. You have a big review meeting with the customer next week. What should you do? Select two answers.**
   a. Present all of the information yourself at the review.
   b. Have only the top technical people on your team attend the review meeting.
   c. Discuss the problem at an all-team meeting.
   d. Discuss the problem with each affected team member individually.

4. **You are heading a new team for an important project within your company. You believe in having a strong team spirit. What should you do? Select two answers.**
   a. Arrange for a team-building session the first day or two on your project.
   b. Create a team name and logo and have all team members wear it on their work badges.
   c. Screen members of your project team to make sure they have a strong team spirit.
   d. Schedule team-building sessions at various times during your project.

5. **Some members of your project team have formed their own group based on their social activities. They always eat lunch together and share many common interests. Unfortunately, they sometimes let their friendships get in the way of accomplishing work on the project. What should you do?**
   a. Talk to the people involved and discuss your concerns.
   b. Insist that the people in this group do not eat lunch together.
   c. Reassign some of the people in this group to other projects.
   d. Make sure people in this group work on the same project tasks.

3.20 Recognize the need to provide leadership that is sensitive to the knowledge, skills, and abilities of team members, and to the corporate culture, while at the same time motivating the team to accomplish the goals defined in the project scope. Recognize and explain the need for a project manager to perform in a manner consistent with a leadership position, adapt leadership style to a specific situation or person, influence or motivate others so that the requirements from a given situation are accomplished, build positive relationships to be accepted as a leader, and provide personal leadership as well as positional leadership.

PROVIDING LEADERSHIP IN A VARIETY OF SITUATIONS

UNDERSTANDING THE OBJECTIVE

The most important trait of good project managers is their ability to lead others. Project managers must be able to adapt to a variety of situations and build relationships.

WHAT YOU REALLY NEED TO KNOW

◆ Project managers must possess leadership skills to be effective. They must provide the vision and inspiration for others to work toward project goals.

◆ Leadership can be personal, meaning people want to follow you because they respect you. Leadership can also be positional, meaning people will follow you because you are in a position of authority.

◆ Project managers must be sensitive to several items in order to be effective leaders:

- Knowledge, skills, and abilities of team members. Some people have a difficult time working with and following leaders. Some team members may need mentoring and personal contact to help them be good followers. It's important for effective project managers to care sincerely about the members of their project team and address their individual knowledge, skills, and abilities.

- The corporate culture. Some companies or organizations have a very distinctive corporate culture that expects leaders to act a certain way. Project managers must understand this culture and perhaps adjust their personal leadership styles to fit into it. Sometimes very strong leaders can use their own unique styles, as long as they produce positive results and do not hurt the existing culture.

◆ Project managers must recognize their role as leaders of their project teams and adapt their style to specific situations or people. Project managers must also be able to influence and motivate others who may not fall under their authority.

◆ An important skill for leaders is the ability to build positive relationships. Project managers must make the time to nurture relationships with key project stakeholders.

OBJECTIVES ON THE JOB

Remember that project managers must lead their teams toward meeting project goals. Building relationships is an important part of being an effective leader and project manager.

PRACTICE TEST QUESTIONS

1. **To what do project managers need to be sensitive in order to be effective leaders? Select two answers.**
   a. the corporate culture
   b. corporate standards
   c. dress codes
   d. individual team members

2. **You have always been fortunate in that people tend to like and respect you as a person. What type of leadership do you naturally possess?**
   a. professional leadership
   b. positional leadership
   c. personality leadership
   d. personal leadership

3. **You were always a very good technical expert on projects, and now you have been promoted to project management. You naturally prefer to focus on specific tasks and technologies and have a difficult time working with people. What type of leadership do you now possess?**
   a. professional leadership
   b. positional leadership
   c. personality leadership
   d. personal leadership

4. **You recently accepted a position as project manager in a new company. This company is known for having a very conservative corporate culture. Your style, however, is to let workers have fun on their jobs. Another project manager has complained to senior management that you are being reckless with funds when you throw a big party for your project team after achieving an important milestone. What should you do?**
   a. Meet with the other manager and senior management to discuss the issue.
   b. Pay for all future team parties with your own funds.
   c. Stop having team parties to celebrate accomplishments.
   d. Nothing.

5. **A senior developer on your project team does not attend many of the team-related activities you plan as leader of your project, such as team lunches, happy hours, and celebrations. The developer is very productive at work but does not enjoy socializing. What should you do?**
   a. Confront the developer and insist he or she attend some of the events.
   b. Drag the worker from his or her desk the next time you have a team social event.
   c. Require the developer to attend a training session on developing social skills.
   d. Nothing.

3.21 Given an initial high level scope, budget, and resource allocation, demonstrate understanding of the need to investigate which aspects of the project could be modified to improve outcomes (i.e., find out what is negotiable, prepare to negotiate). Provide evidence of the following competencies: recognition that individual project team members' needs must be addressed to the extent that project activities can be modified without significant impact on final scope, budget, quality, or schedule; the ability to evaluate alternatives to a scope change request that stakeholders may find acceptable; the ability to recognize which aspects (schedule, budget, quality) of the project are most important to the stakeholders and be able to propose trade-offs during the project that can be made to meet or exceed those aspects; and the ability to identify all of the individuals and groups with which you will need to negotiate during the life of the project.

NEGOTIATING TO IMPROVE PROJECT OUTCOMES

UNDERSTANDING THE OBJECTIVE

It is important to make sure project outcomes are realistic and achievable. Project managers need to manage and negotiate resources throughout the life of a project.

WHAT YOU REALLY NEED TO KNOW

- ◆ Various aspects of information technology projects change during the course of the project. It is important for project managers to sense what can be negotiated and what cannot, in order to produce a positive outcome.

- ◆ Project team members are crucial resources. Project managers must work with individual team members to meet their individual needs and the needs of the project. For example, there may be situations where the project manager needs to ask an individual to reschedule a vacation or work on something he or she doesn't like to do in order to meet project goals. In turn, the project manager might provide an extra day of vacation or authorize a special training course for the individual.

- ◆ Stakeholders often want to change the scope of a project. Project managers must work with their teams to negotiate scope changes that are in the best interests of the organization. They must identify and propose trade-offs between changes in scope and effects on quality, time, and cost goals.

- ◆ Project managers must be aware of all the people involved in or affected by their projects and know when negotiations are needed.

OBJECTIVES ON THE JOB

Understand that negotiating is an important part of a project manager's job.

PRACTICE TEST QUESTIONS

1. **With whom might project managers need to negotiate while managing a project? Select three answers.**
   - a. team members
   - b. vendors
   - c. users
   - d. quality control

2. **You have just been given a draft contract from a company providing products and services for a large information technology project. What should you do?**
   - a. Sign and return it as soon as possible.
   - b. Review the contract and decide what you think should be negotiated.
   - c. Ignore the standard contract and send your own contract back to them.
   - d. Hire a lawyer to interpret and negotiate the contract for you.

3. **You have lost several talented software developers on your project. Your team has decided to outsource some of the development work. You have received a proposal from a respected firm, but their price seems high. What should you do?**
   - a. Offer to pay what it would cost to do the work internally.
   - b. Try to negotiate the price.
   - c. Refuse the proposal and look for a different source.
   - d. Hire a professional negotiator to get you the developers you need.

4. **Your developers are complaining that the users keep changing the scope of what they what done on your project, causing more work for the project team. The senior developer has a hard time saying no to any user requests. What should you do? Select two answers.**
   - a. Propose trade-offs in order to meet project scope, time, and cost goals.
   - b. Provide estimates of the additional time and money required for these scope changes.
   - c. Have a nontechnical person who is good at negotiating talk to the users.
   - d. Do not allow any scope changes to the project.

5. **What should be the primary focus of project managers when managing their projects?**
   - a. keeping their project team happy
   - b. keeping the project sponsor happy
   - c. meeting project goals
   - d. staying within budget

Domain IV

4.1   Recognize and explain the value of conducting a comprehensive review process that evaluates the planning, organizing, directing, controlling, execution, and budget phases of the project, identifying both the positive and the negative aspects in a written report.

CONDUCTING A COMPREHENSIVE PROJECT REVIEW

UNDERSTANDING THE OBJECTIVE

When projects end, it is important to conduct a review that evaluates various phases of the project. Stakeholders should discuss and documents positive and negative aspects of the project in a written report.

WHAT YOU REALLY NEED TO KNOW

◆ It is important for people to learn from the past. When projects near completion, the team should take the time to conduct a comprehensive review of the project.

◆ The project review should evaluate various phases of the project, including planning, organizing, directing, controlling, executing, and budgeting.

◆ When closing projects, it is important to prepare **project archives** to leave clear and complete documentation of the project.

◆ If projects involve contracts, the contracts must be closed out. Contract files should document formal acceptance and closure of the work done for the project.

◆ People often learn most from their mistakes. In addition to documenting facts and what went right on a project, it is important to document what went wrong to help avoid making the same mistakes in the future.

◆ Project teams often document what they learned from projects in a **lessons learned** report. Future project teams can benefit from reading the lessons learned reports of others. Some organizations require new project managers to review lessons learned from previous projects so that they can learn from past mistakes.

◆ Some projects perform a **project audit**. The goal of a project audit is a formal review of project progress and results. The main questions addressed in a project audit include:

- Did the project achieve the benefits as planned?

- Was the work accomplished according to plan?

OBJECTIVES ON THE JOB

Take the time to close out projects formally. It will help you and future project teams.

PRACTICE TEST QUESTIONS

1. **What types of documents are created to provide a clear and complete documentation of a project's history?**
   a. contracts
   b. lessons learned
   c. project audit
   d. project archives

2. **Match the following items to their descriptions.**

   Lessons learned   a.   Leave a clear and complete history of a project
   Project audits   b.   Review project progress and results
   Project archives   c.   Document what went right or wrong on a project

3. **What are the main questions addressed in a project audit? Select two answers.**
   a. Did the project achieve the planned benefits?
   b. Were project funds spent as planned?
   c. Did the project team follow corporate policies and procedures?
   d. Was the project work accomplished according to plan?

4. **Your project is nearing completion, and everyone is relieved. Many things did not go well on the project, and people are looking forward to new assignments. Your project sponsor has asked your team to prepare a presentation and written report documenting lessons learned. What should you include in this report? Select two answers.**
   a. what went right
   b. what went wrong
   c. who did a good job
   d. who did a bad job

5. **Your project is nearing completion, and everyone is relieved. Many things did not go well on the project, and people are looking forward to new assignments. Your project sponsor has asked your team to prepare a presentation and written report documenting lessons learned. People don't want to participate since they might look bad. What should you do?**
   a. Prepare the presentation and report yourself.
   b. Tell the project sponsor that you did not budget for this activity and that project personnel have already been reassigned.
   c. Work with the project team to prepare the lessons learned, being sensitive to individual needs.

6. **Your organization requires everyone to write a lessons learned report at the end of major projects, but the same mistakes are made repeatedly. What strategy could your company use for better sharing of lessons learned?**
   a. Require everyone to put the lessons learned information on the Web.
   b. Have weekly meetings to discuss lessons learned.
   c. Require new project managers to read lessons learned reports from past projects and discuss what they can do to prevent making similar mistakes.

Domain I
Objective 1.1
Practice Questions:
1. a,b,d
2. d
3. a
4. c,a,d,b
5. c
6. b,c
7. b

Objective 1.2
Practice Questions:
1. c
2. a,b,d
3. d
4. b,d
5. a,c
6. a,c,e

Objective 1.3
Practice Questions:
1. a
2. a,b,d
3. c
4. a,b
5. d,a,b,c
6. c

Objective 1.4
Practice Questions:
1. a,b,d
2. d
3. b,d
4. b,c
5. d,a,b,e,c
6. c

Objective 1.5
Practice Questions:
1. a,b
2. a,c
3. a
4. a,d
5. a,c

Objective 1.5 (cont.)
Practice Questions:
1. a
2. a,b,d
3. b
4. a,b,d
5. a,b
6. a

Objective 1.6
Practice Questions:
1. a,b,e
2. a,d
3. b
4. b
5. a,c

Objective 1.7
Practice Questions:
1. a,c
2. d
3. b
4. b
5. b
6. b,d

Objective 1.8
Practice Questions:
1. c
2. a,d
3. b
4. a
5. b
6. a,b

Objective 1.9
Practice Questions:
1. a,c,d
2. b,d
3. b,c
4. a,d
5. a
6. c

Objective 1.10

Practice Questions:

1. b
2. d
3. b,c
4. c
5. b,c
6. b

Objective 1.11

Practice Questions:

1. a,c,e
2. a,c
3. a
4. b,d,a,c
5. c,d

Objective 1.12

Practice Questions:

1. b
2. b,c,d
3. b,c,d
4. d
5. b,c
6. c

Objective 1.13

Practice Questions:

1. b
2. a,b
3. c
4. a,d
5. b,c
6. c,d

Objective 1.14

Practice Questions:

1. d
2. b,c
3. a,b,d
4. a,c
5. a,b,c
6. a,b

Domain II
Objective 2.1
Practice Questions:
1. c
2. a,d
3. a,b,d
4. b,d,c,a
5. a,c,d
6. a,c

Objective 2.2
Practice Questions:
1. a,b,d
2. b,c,a
3. b
4. a,c
5. c
6. b

Objective 2.2 (cont.)
Practice Questions:
1. b,c
2. c,d
3. b
4. a
5. a,b
6. b

Objective 2.3
Practice Questions:
1. a,b,d
2. d
3. c
4. a
5. b
6. b

Objective 2.4
Practice Questions:
1. b
2. c
3. a,c
4. a
5. d
6. a,b

Objective 2.5

Practice Questions:

1. c
2. b
3. c
4. a,c
5. b

Objective 2.6

Practice Questions:

1. a
2. d,c,e,a,b
3. c
4. a
5. c
6. a

Objective 2.7

Practice Questions:

1. b,d
2. a,d
3. a
4. a
5. a,b

Objective 2.8

Practice Questions:

1. d
2. a,c,d
3. a,d
4. b
5. a,b

Objective 2.9

Practice Questions:

1. d
2. c,a,b
3. c
4. b
5. a,c
6. c

Objective 2.10

Practice Questions:

1. a,c,d
2. a,d
3. a,c
4. c
5. a
6. d

Objective 2.11

Practice Questions:

1. d
2. b,d
3. c
4. a,b,d
5. a,c,d
6. d

Objective 2.12

Practice Questions:

1. b,c,d
2. a,c
3. b
4. c,a,b,d
5. b,d
6. c

Objective 2.13

Practice Questions:

1. a,b,e
2. b,d
3. a,c
4. a,b,d
5. a,d

Objective 2.14

Practice Questions:

1. d
2. c
3. a
4. a
5. a
6. a,b,d

Objective 2.15

Practice Questions:

1. d
2. a,b,d
3. b,d
4. a,c
5. a,d
6. a,c

Objective 2.16

Practice Questions:

1. c
2. b
3. a,d
4. d
5. a
6. c

Objective 2.17

Practice Questions:

1. a,d,e
2. a
3. a,b,d
4. c
5. b
6. b,c,d

Objective 2.18

Practice Questions:

1. a,c,d
2. a,d
3. a,d
4. c
5. a
6. d

Objective 2.19

Practice Questions:

1. b,c,d
2. a,d
3. d
4. c
5. d
6. b,c

ANSWER KEY

Objective 2.20
Practice Questions:
1. a,c,d
2. c
3. a,d
4. a,d
5. c

Objective 2.21
Practice Questions:
1. a,b,c
2. c
3. c
4. c
5. b
6. a

Objective 2.22
Practice Questions:
1. a,b,d
2. c
3. a
4. a,c
5. b,c
6. c

Objective 2.23
Practice Questions:
1. b,c,d,e,a,f
2. a,b,d
3. a,d
4. b,d
5. a,b,d
6. a,d

Domain III
Objective 3.1
Practice Questions:
1. a,b,d
2. d
3. a,c
4. b,c
5. a,d
6. a,c

Objective 3.2
Practice Questions:
1. c,d,e
2. a,b,d
3. b
4. a,d
5. a,c,d

Objective 3.3
Practice Questions:
1. a,c
2. c,d
3. a,b
4. a
5. a,b
6. b

Objective 3.4
Practice Questions:
1. a,c,d
2. b,c,d
3. a
4. a
5. a,c
6. c

Objective 3.5
Practice Questions:
1. b
2. d
3. a,b,c
4. a
5. b,d

Objective 3.6
Practice Questions:
1. a,b,c
2. b,d
3. a
4. a,d
5. c

Objective 3.7
Practice Questions:
1. b,d
2. d
3. a
4. c
5. a
6. d

Objective 3.8
Practice Questions:
1. b,c
2. a,b
3. a,c,d
4. a
5. d
6. c,d

Objective 3.9
Practice Questions:
1. a,d,e
2. b
3. c
4. b,c
5. c,d
6. b

Objective 3.10
Practice Questions:
1. b
2. b
3. b,c
4. a,b,c
5. a
6. a,b,d

Objective 3.11
Practice Questions:
1. b,c,d
2. a,d
3. d
4. d,b,a,c
5. b,d

Objective 3.12

Practice Questions:

1. a,d
2. b,c,d
3. d
4. b,c,d
5. b
6. a,b

Objective 3.13

Practice Questions:

1. d,b,c,a
2. b,c,d
3. b
4. b
5. d
6. c

Objective 3.14

Practice Questions:

1. a,c
2. c
3. b
4. a,c,d
5. a,c

Objective 3.15

Practice Questions:

1. b,c
2. a
3. a
4. b
5. c

Objective 3.16

Practice Questions:

1. b
2. d
3. c,b,d,a
4. a,b,d
5. b,c,d

Objective 3.17

Practice Questions:

1. a
2. a,c
3. a,b,d
4. b
5. d

Objective 3.18
Practice Questions:
1. a,d
2. d
3. c
4. c,d
5. c

Objective 3.19
Practice Questions:
1. a,b
2. b,c
3. c,d
4. a,d
5. a

Objective 3.20
Practice Questions:
1. a,d
2. d
3. b
4. a
5. d

Objective 3.21
Practice Questions:
1. a,b,c
2. b
3. b
4. a,b
5. c

Domain IV
Objective 4.1
Practice Questions:
1. d
2. c,b,a
3. a,d
4. a,b
5. c
6. c

INDEX

H

helpdesk training, 110–111
hierarchy format, 62–63
human resource managers,
114–115, 120

I

implementation plans, 78–79
industry regulations, 16–17, 24–25
integration, 42–43, 108–109
interviews, 28–29, 44–45
ISO (International Standards
Organization), 16
iteration, planning for, 60–61

J

Joint Application Design (JAD), 102

K

key assumptions, 12–13
kick-off meetings, 28–29

L

leadership, providing, 122–123
lessons learned reports, 128–129

M

management. *See also* project managers;
senior managers
of budgets, 12–13, 56–57
buy-in, 30–31
reserves, 12–13
risk, 54–55
mandatory dependencies, 36–37
meetings, 28–29
memos, 28–29
methodologies, 16–17, 24–25
metrics, 34–35
milestones, 38–39, 58–59, 66–69,
106–107
mistakes, learning form, 128–129
morale, 76–77

N

negotiation, 28–29, 124–125
network diagrams, 36–39, 58–59

O

organizational structures, types of, 18–19
overtime periods, 118–119

P

parametric modeling, 40–41
percent complete (PV), 96–97
performance feedback, providing,
112–113
performance problems
among unfocused/fragmented teams,
120–121
handling individual, 116–117
personality clashes, 76–77
PERT charts, 38–39, 53
primary drivers, 2
priorities, of projects, 8–9, 14–15
progress reports, 34–35
project(s). *See also* projects managers
archives, 128
audits, 128–129
charters, 3–4, 6–7
closing, 128–129
concept definition, 2–3
justification of, 10
killing, deciding the necessity of,
84–85
management software, 58–59
organization, 18–19
outcomes, negotiating to improve,
124–125
plans, 8–9, 14–15, 34–35, 60–61,
78–81
quality management plans, 42–43
reviews, 128–129
status, reporting, 84–85
project manager(s)
basic description of, 2
budgets and, 12–13
building consensus and, 28–29
change control and, 100–101
communication skills and, 92–93
disgruntled employees and, 114–115
executive support and, 6–7, 92–93
good communications and, 76–77
handling performance problems and,
116–117
leadership skills and, 122–123

maintaining qualified deliverables
and, 106–107
overtime periods and, 118–119
project goals and, 14–15
role of, identifying, 18–19
scope changes and, 104–105
scope definitions and, 24–25
unfocused/fragmented teams and,
120–121
vendor delays and, 88–89

Q

qualitative risk analysis, 54–55
quality
control, 42–43, 106–107, 110–111
expected from vendors, 90
management, 42–43, 108–109
planning, 42–43

R

recognition, providing, 118–119
regulations, 16–17, 24–25
requirement(s)
business, 2–3, 52–53
change control process, 26–27
decomposing, while maintaining
traceability, 52–53
developing, 10–11
evaluating, 48–49
in project plans, 78–79
reviews, 50–51
of specific industry regulations,
16–17
resource(s)
availability, 70–75
expected, identifying, in project plans,
78–79
good communications and, 76–77
responsibilities, 18–19, 34–35, 64
risk(s)
defining customer expectations
and, 8–9
identifying potential, 54–55
management planning, 54–55
mitigation, 54–55
roles, identifying, 18–19
rough order of magnitude (ROM),
40–41